THE STANLEY BOOK OF
WOODWORK

TOOLS | TECHNIQUES | PROJECTS

MARK FINNEY

BATSFORD

First published 1994
Reprinted 1994, 1997, 2000, 2001
This edition published 2006

Volume © B T Batsford 1994, 2006
Text © Mark Finney 1994, 2006
Furniture designs and working drawings © Mark Finney 1994, 2006
Illustrations © Sandra Pond and Will Giles 1994, 2006
Photographs © Stanley Tools
Photography by Latent Image, Sheffield 1994

ISBN-13 9780713490039
ISBN-10 0 7134 9003 9

A CIP catalogue record for this book is available from the
British Library.

Printed in Singapore by Kyodo Printing Co. Ltd
for the publishers:

B T Batsford
Chrysalis Books Group
The Chrysalis Building
Bramley Road
London W10 6SP
www.chrysalisbooks.co.uk

Distributed in the United States and Canada by Sterling Publishing Co.,
387 Park Avenue South, New York, NY 10016, USA

DISCLAIMER:
Some tools have been included to show a specific type of tool or
technique and, although they may no longer be manufactured, they
are still likely to be found in a typical tool kit.

CONTENTS

Foreword 5
How to use this book 6
Conversion chart 7
Making a start 8
The materials 12

TOOLS 17 Measuring and marking out tools 18
Saws 24
Planes 30
Hammers and mallets 39
Chisels 42
Hand drills and braces 46
Screwdrivers 50
Tools used for holding 54
Caring for your tool kit 58

TECHNIQUES 63 Marking out 64
Planing 70
Cutting and fitting joints 76
Assembling and gluing up 89
Finishing 100

PROJECTS 109 How to use this section 110
Woodwork bench 112
Bookcase 118
Child's desk 126
Chest 134
Bedside cabinet 142
Small table with drawer 150

Useful addresses and further reading 158
Index 159

FOREWORD

There is little more truly satisfying than taking a piece of raw timber and transforming it into a beautiful, functional piece of furniture. Working with fine quality hand tools, and learning to use them to make the most of wood's natural strength and enhance its beauty, makes for particularly rewarding woodwork.

We at STANLEY have been producing the finest quality hand tools for over 150 years. Starting from modest beginnings in the United States, we have developed over the last century and a half into the world's leading hand tools manufacturer. Our basic philosophy has been the driving and sustaining force throughout: to us, quality and integrity are essential in all things. Phenomenal effort goes into developing and testing every single tool we make to ensure its quality, precision and suitability for the job.

We live in an age where, in almost all walks of life, modern machine methods are taking over from traditional hand techniques. Power tools and machines in woodworking certainly give good results, but there will always be a place for hand skills, and by taking the time to learn how to use the tools to their best effect, you will give yourself an excellent basis for all kinds of woodworking.

As one of the world's best tool companies, we are proud to have joined with one of the world's best woodworking publishers to produce a book that is packed with information, is presented in a lively, friendly and easy-to-use design, and really teaches you all you need either to start woodworking from scratch, or to improve your basic skills. Even if you have never picked up a chisel in your life, by the time you reach the end of this book you will be able to make six pieces of furniture ranging from basic to more advanced – and, what's more important, you should have had a good deal of pleasure on the way.

Enjoy your woodworking!

STANLEY TOOLS

HOW TO USE THIS BOOK

In a world where there seems to be a machine that will do just about anything, do hand tools for woodwork still have an important role to play? The answer is a resounding yes! Tried and tested techniques, perfected generations ago, are still used today and will continue to be used for many years to come.

Traditional hand tools are efficient and simple shapers of wood, guaranteeing accuracy every time, if they are used properly.

The aim of this book is to show you the tools that build up a tool kit and to explain how to use them; to take you through the techniques for preparing wood, marking out and cutting joints, assembling furniture and finishing. At the back of the book there are projects that have been specially designed to put into practice some of the skills you have learned.

In woodwork there are often several, equally valid, ways of doing things, and experienced woodworkers will always have their own favourite methods. If anyone tells you that there is another way than the one described in this book, then all to the good – if woodwork is to survive and develop then the sharing and passing on of ideas and knowledge is crucial. What I can guarantee is that all the techniques explained in this book work – and if you follow these instructions you will enjoy safe and satisfying woodwork.

As you go through this book you will find basic instructions for woodworking, and all sorts of tips, advice, technical talk boxes and shopping guides. At the beginning of each section you will find a practical explanation of things contained within it and there are some general points too, that are appropriate throughout the whole book.

OLD TOOLS

In the Tools section of this book you will find shopping guides which will tell you what it is essential to buy if you are building up your tool kit from scratch. You may already have an old tool kit handed on to you by a father or grandfather, or one you had at school, or just a collection pulled together from all sorts of miscellaneous places. Do remember that all hand tools, especially old ones, must be suitable for the job for which you want to use them. Just because a tool is old, it does not necessarily mean that it is better quality or will perform better. Always check the soles of planes for flatness, marking out equipment for accuracy and ensure your saw blades are sharp and straight.

RIGHT- AND LEFT-HANDED WOODWORKERS

For the sake of simplicity and space, the instructions in this book for holding tools and for woodwork techniques assume that the woodworker is right-handed. If, however, you are left-handed, you do not need special left-handed tools – simply reverse the hands described in the instructions accordingly.

PRACTISING

If you are unsure of a technique, use scrap pieces of wood to practise on first. If you are to practise successfully, it is vital that you take proper time and care to prepare the wood correctly, even if it is to be thrown away afterwards. If you are practising finishing it is especially important to make sure that the wood samples are planed and sanded to the same standard as a finished project.

CONVERSION CHART

Depending on where you are in the world you may be used to metric or imperial measurements, or both. This chart gives you exact conversions for reference, though bear in mind that in practice, and throughout the text of this book, very small degrees of measurement are usually rounded up or down – so, for example, the equivalent to a ¼in drill bit appears as 6mm, as it is sold, not 6.4mm, which is the exact conversion. However, there will be occasions when an exact conversion is desirable.

mm	in	mm	in	mm	in	mm	in	mm	in
0.40	$1/64$	10.32	$13/32$	20.24	$51/64$	330.2	13	965.2	38
0.79	$1/32$	10.72	$27/64$	20.64	$13/16$	355.6	14	990.6	39
1.19	$3/64$	11.11	$7/16$	21.03	$53/64$	381	15	101.6	40
1.59	$1/16$	11.51	$29/64$	21.43	$27/32$	406.4	16	1041.4	41
1.98	$5/64$	11.91	$15/32$	21.83	$55/64$	431.8	17	1066.8	42
2.38	$3/32$	12.30	$31/64$	22.23	$7/8$	457.2	18	1092.2	43
2.78	$7/64$	12.70	$1/2$	22.62	$57/64$	482.6	19	1117.6	44
3.18	$1/8$	13.10	$33/64$	23.02	$29/32$	508	20	1143	45
3.57	$9/64$	13.49	$17/32$	23.42	$59/64$	533.4	21	1168.4	46
3.97	$5/32$	13.89	$35/64$	23.81	$15/16$	558.8	22	1193.8	47
4.37	$11/64$	14.29	$9/16$	24.21	$61/64$	584.2	23	1219.2	48
4.76	$3/16$	14.68	$37/64$	24.61	$31/32$	609.6	24	1244.6	49
5.16	$13/64$	15.08	$19/32$	25	$63/64$	635	25	1270	50
5.56	$7/32$	15.48	$39/64$	25.4	1	660.4	26	1295.4	51
5.95	$15/64$	15.88	$5/8$	50.8	2	685.8	27	1320.8	52
6.35	$1/4$	16.27	$41/64$	76.2	3	711.2	28	1346.2	53
6.75	$17/64$	16.67	$21/32$	101.6	4	736.6	29	1371.6	54
7.14	$9/32$	17.07	$43/64$	127	5	762	30	1397	55
7.54	$19/64$	17.46	$11/16$	152.4	6	787.4	31	1422.4	56
7.94	$5/16$	17.86	$45/64$	177.8	7	812.8	32	1447.8	57
8.33	$21/64$	18.26	$23/32$	203.2	8	838.2	33	1473.2	58
8.73	$11/32$	18.65	$47/64$	228.6	9	863.6	34	1498.6	59
9.13	$23/64$	19.05	$3/4$	254	10	889	35	1524	60
9.53	$3/8$	19.45	$49/64$	279.4	11	914.4	36	1549.4	61
9.92	$25/64$	19.88	$25/32$	304.8	12	939.8	37	1574.8	62

MAKING A START

First you need enthusiasm, patience and a willingness to learn from the mistakes you will inevitably make.

THE WORKSHOP

Your workplace might be anything from a corner of a garage to a fully kitted out workshop. If you have a choice, look for somewhere with a good daylight source and with good ventilation. An even more important thing to consider is the dryness (or wetness) of the workplace, as this will affect the stability of the wood itself.

Workshop Equipment

You should always work on a flat, undamaged surface, and so the first essential is a well-made workbench preferably with a vice (see page 54). The first project in this book, on page 112, is a good, simple workbench design.

Overalls or a woodworker's apron will protect your clothes from dust, glue and spillages – those with a large pocket in the front for holding pencils and tape measures are particularly useful, but do not keep sharp knives or chisels in them. It could be very dangerous if you bend down.

A dust cover, or old sheet, is useful for covering up other pieces of work, especially if they have been polished, when you are sanding or machining.

UNDERSTANDING THE MATERIALS

Moisture in Wood

Wood is hygroscopic, which means that as a material, it will either absorb or lose moisture to the damper or drier atmosphere that surrounds it. This may take a few hours or several days to happen, but if it does, the wood will expand as it becomes wetter or shrink as it dries – witness the door that sticks in wet weather.

For woodworkers, most problems with moisture in wood occur as you move it from one place to another, for example from an outdoor workshop into your living room, or straight from the timber yard to near a hot radiator. In extreme cases this may result in warping, cracks and splits. It makes no difference how long a tree has been felled, as the wood will always try to recondition itself to its new environment. So, for example, an older piece of furniture stored outdoors will absorb moisture from the air, resulting in each component slowly expanding, perhaps even pulling the joints apart as it does so.

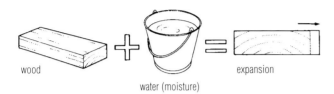

wood + water (moisture) = expansion

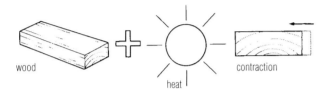

wood + heat = contraction

Wood is hygroscopic:
it expands or contracts as it gains or loses moisture

HOW TO LOOK AFTER WOOD

Let us assume you have bought dry wood from a timber yard. If you work on it for a few days in a workshop that is damp, the wood will expand in the workshop and then contract again later when the wood is brought indoors to a drier environment. It is wise, therefore, to keep wood in surroundings as similar as possible to where it will be finally placed, taking pieces to the workshop only when they are needed. When you have finished working on them, bring them back to their drier environment – even accidentally leaving the wood in a damp workshop overnight can cause it to swell slightly and possibly distort. If your workshop is dry, of course, or is about the same moisture content as indoors, there should not be a problem and you can store the wood there safely.

IMPORTANT

Make sure you do not confuse coldness in a workshop with dampness.

CUTTING MATERIALS TO SIZE

Before starting a project you may need to cut long lengths of wood or sheet materials down to more manageable sizes.

It is important to provide support to the wood (including the waste) for both safety and to prevent damage.

CROSSCUTTING

Solid wood may need cutting to length (crosscutting) ready for work to commence. Here a crosscut saw (see page 24) is used. Support the wood as shown.

RIPPING BOARDS ALONG THEIR LENGTH

If you are to rip the wood along its length, a slightly longer saw is more appropriate but it must be capable of sawing along the grain (see page 25).

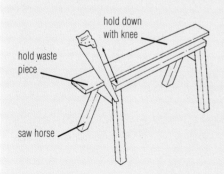

hold down with knee

hold waste piece

saw horse

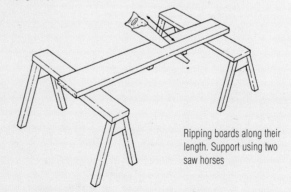

Ripping boards along their length. Support using two saw horses

NOTE: Sheet materials should be held on two saw horses, making sure that the waste is properly supported so that it does not flap during sawing. Very thin sheets can be laid on two lengths of timber, placed across both saw horses on either side and parallel to the intended saw cut. When cutting sheet materials, stop them from moving around by using your knee if necessary and use a relaxed stroke to saw along a marked line. If the saw binds in the saw cut, try using a little candle wax to lubricate the blade, and gently wedge open the kerf (saw cut) with a small wedge to give the saw more clearance (see also page 129).

AIR DRYING A natural and quite slow method of reducing the moisture content of green (freshly felled) wood, taking about one year to dry 25mm (1in) thick hardwood planking

CHOCKS Lengths of wood of larger section than sticking laths used to raise the wood from the ground during drying.

HYGROSCOPIC Absorbing or losing moisture according to the moisture content of the environment and thus changing dimensionally, which can cause problems of distortion or cracking

KILN DRYING A faster artificial method where the wood is placed in a chamber, taking one to two weeks to dry 25mm (1in) thick hardwood planking

SECONDARY CONDITIONING The stabilizing of previously dried wood prior to being worked

SOLE (of a plane) The base of the plane, on which it runs

STICKING LATHS Small pieces of wood of uniform thickness used to separate planks of wood during drying

WARPING Movement of wood: the four types are bow, cup, twist and spring (see page 14)

SECONDARY CONDITIONING

Before using newly purchased wood it is preferable to secondary condition, particularly if you are to use it for important joinery or furniture. Secondary conditioning will help to stabilize the wood. This is necessary because the moisture content of new wood is generally higher than that of, say, a centrally heated room, and to avoid problems occurring later on, you should, ideally, try to make one match the other.

HOW TO SECONDARY CONDITION WOOD

There are several important points to remember which will help to keep the timber flat and stable.

- Store the wood in an environment similar to that where you will put the finished furniture

- Remember that whether it has been air-dried or kiln-dried at the timber yard, solid wood should still be secondary conditioned before use

- If you cut the wood to the approximate sizes needed before secondary conditioning, the entire process will be speeded up. This will also make handling the wood easier

- Use pieces of wood of equal thickness for the sticking laths. These are used to separate the wood, providing ventilation helping it to dry out. Place sticking laths between the planks and directly in line on top of each other. The laths should never be further apart than 380mm (15in) or the boards may sag

- Put weights on the top boards over a row of sticking laths to keep them flat

- Secondary conditioning will take around two to three weeks for 25mm (1in) thick softwood and three to four weeks for 25mm (1in) thick hardwood at an average room temperature – longer for thicker planks.

During the secondary conditioning process, wood must be correctly stored

weights on top planks will keep wood flat

weight supports

all laths and blocks on a row must be of equal thickness and stacked on top of each other in line

blocks/chocks

sticking laths minimum 13mm (½in) thick

timber cut to approximate dimensions

SAFETY IN THE WORKSHOP

With traditional hand tools and skills, there may well be more likelihood of you damaging the wood than yourself! However, accidents can happen and you must take precautions to avoid injury. Look after your fingers and eyes in particular, and always have a first aid box to hand.

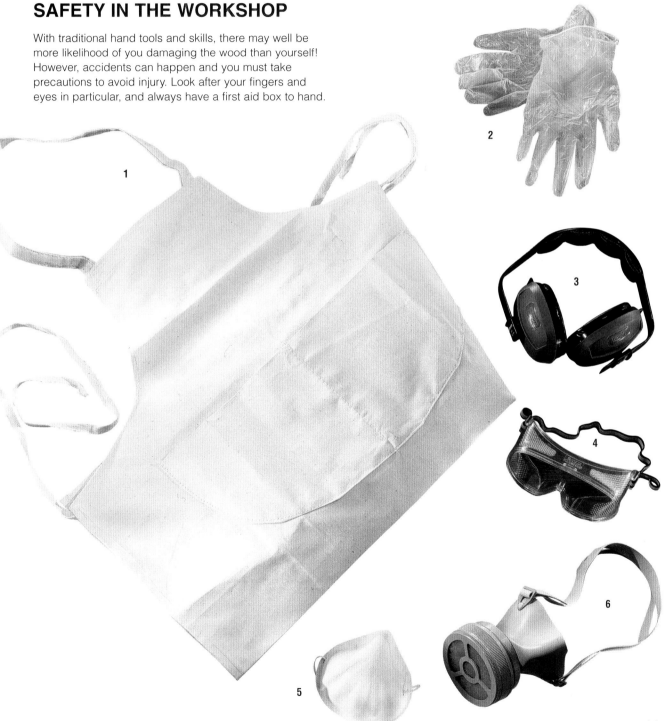

GOLDEN RULES

- When using sharp hand tools, such as chisels, always push the blade away from you, so that if you slip you will not cut yourself

- Never wear jewellery or loose-fitting clothes. Tie back your hair if necessary when in the workshop

- Wear suitable ear, nose and eye defenders when appropriate

- When finishing, always open a window for ventilation. Some materials commonly used in woodwork give off strong odours or are highly flammable

- Always store stains and polishes safely and away from children

- If at any time when you are using a tool, you do not feel in complete control, always stop! If you are using a tool correctly it should feel comfortable, so re-read the instructions and try again

1 Woodworker's apron with pouch
2 Safety gloves
3 Ear defenders
4 Safety goggles
5 Dust mask
6 Dust respirator

11

THE MATERIALS

GOOD ADVICE

Trees yield wood of varying qualities which are then graded. Always ask the advice of a good timber merchant when deciding which grade of wood you should select for your project. Any timber to be used for quality work should have been suitably dried before purchase.

TIP

Wood is often sold with the bark still on it. This is known as a waney-edged board. Although prices may seem cheaper, don't forget that there will be considerably more waste. (See page 23 for converting waney-edged boards.)

One of the real joys of working in wood is that wood is a living material, a renewable resource, and since every tree is different, so is every piece of wood.

HARDWOODS AND SOFTWOODS

There are over 35,000 species of hardwood and around 200 species of softwood throughout the world. Most of these are not suitable for general woodwork: some trees are far too small or too sparse to produce recognizable commercial timbers. Where several timbers are similar to each other they may be grouped together for sale as a mixed species. The mahogany substitutes (such as lauan) fall into this category and this accounts for the wide range of shades within a single batch of wood. The timbers listed are some of the most popular among woodworkers: all are readily available.

What is the difference between hardwoods and softwoods? Although in most cases hardwoods are actually harder and tougher than softwoods, the real difference between the two is that in general, softwoods originate from cone-bearing trees and hardwoods from trees that have their seeds contained in a seed-case (so an apple tree is therefore a hardwood).

Hardwoods can in actual fact vary from being very hard (greenheart, for example, is particularly dense and tough) to extremely soft (obeche and balsa wood are both hardwoods). Some hardwoods are so heavy that they are unable to float in water! Softwoods, meanwhile, are not necessarily soft – parana pine from South America is actually harder and tougher than many hardwoods.

A good guide to the strength of each timber is the density figure showing kg/m³. Generally, the higher this figure is, the tougher and harder the wood. To gauge how heavy a wood is, compare its density to that of water, which is 1000kg/m³.

Softwoods

Douglas Fir
Pseudotsuga menziesii – 530kg/m³.
From North America, Britain
Light brown with reddish tone. Attractive, bold figure. Better grades suitable for quality work and lower grades for constructional use and plywoods. May surface check while being dried.

Parana Pine
Araucaria angustifolia – 550kg/m³.
From South America
Pale to mid-golden-brown, often with red streaks. Suitable for top quality interior work. Very hard and decorative but has a tendency to distort badly if it is not correctly dried and conditioned before use.

Quebec Yellow Pine
Pinus strobus – 420kg/m³.
From North America
Straw brown, very stable softwood often used for detailed mouldings and patterns. It is an easily workable, fine-textured timber. Can be used for model making and carving.

Redwood
(also called European redwood, pine, Scots pine, Baltic redwood): *Pinus sylvestris* - 510kg/m³.
Best grades from Scandinavia/Russia
Pale yellow to orange/light brown. Depending on the grade, redwood can be used for jobs varying from top quality joinery and furniture, through to construction work. Can be a resinous timber, sometimes making it difficult to work. Polishes well, but may take wood stain patchily.

Southern Yellow Pine
(also called Southern pine): mixed species of *Pinus palustris, Pinus elliotti, Pinus echinata, Pinus taeda* - 560kg/m³. From southern USA
Includes pitch pine which is light brown with a yellow/

orange tone. It has a strong figure, resembling that of Douglas fir. The best grades are suitable for furniture and lower grades for constructional work, plywood and joinery.

Whitewood

(also called European whitewood – mix of silver fir and spruce): Picea spp., especially *Picea abies* and *Abies alba* – 400-500kg/m³.
From Europe, Scandinavia, Russia
White/pale yellow. Good for constructional work and more economical joinery. Small, dark, dead knots, have a tendency to fall out on drying. Does not work, stain and polish as attractively as redwood.

Western Red Cedar

Thuja plicata - 390kg/m³.
From North America
Reddish/brown softwood with a pleasant scent. Western red cedar is very easy to work, but is a little soft, so damages easily. A very attractive and stable timber used for making roof shingles (wooden tiles), for exterior claddings, light constructional work and beehives.

Hardwoods

Ash, American White

Fraxinus spp. - 670kg/m³.
From USA
White/pale brown, attractive, open-textured, ring-porous timber that works, stains and polishes well. Used for furniture or components that need to be tough, e.g. tool handles. Ash can be steam bent and laminated.

Beech, European

Fagus sylvatica - 720kg/m³.
From Europe
Available unsteamed (white beech) and steamed (sterilized to stop it discolouring – pink beech). Strong, tough, close-textured timber, rather bland appearance. For furniture, drawer sides, flooring, plywood, mallets and woodwork benches.

Cherry, American

(also called Pennsylvanian black cherry): *Prunus serotina* – 580-620kg/m³.
From USA

Heartwood darkens rapidly on exposure to sunlight to an attractive pinkish brown. Superb, fine-looking wood used for furniture, cabinet and decorative work. It is very close-textured and polishes well.

Iroko

(also called African teak): *Chlorophora excelsa* - 660kg/m³.
From West Africa
Golden brown, very durable timber which can be used as an alternative to teak. Suitable for exterior/interior joinery and furniture. Always wear a face mask when cutting and sanding because of irritant dust. Not usually available from sustainable sources.

Mahogany, Brazilian

Swietenia macrophylla - 560kg/m³.
From Central and South America, primarily Brazil
Pale red/brown wood, often with no strong or marked figures. It stains and polishes well. Stocks are often not from sustainable sources. Substitutes include West African mahogany, dark red lauan and some species from Papua New Guinea. True mahogany is expensive, so any wood that has a similar grain, figure and colour, is often in demand as an alternative. Most often used for internal joinery, furniture, doors and windows. Other alternatives with a more stripy figure include sapele and utile.

Maple, Hard

(also called hard rock maple, rock maple, sugar maple): *Acer saccharum* - 740kg/m³.
From North America
White/creamy-white hardwood, sometimes with a slight pale-grey discoloration. Fine-textured, hard timber. Does not have a strong figure. Very resistant to impact and abrasion. Works and polishes well. Suitable for flooring, sports goods, furniture and interior joinery.

Oak, American White

Quercus spp. - 770kg/m³.
From North America
Pale to mid-brown/grey. A different species from European oak, which is easier to work and a little browner in colour. Traditionally used for making barrels, it is now a top quality furniture and cabinet-making timber. Stains and polishes well. Iron will react and mark the wood in damp conditions, so always use brass or stainless steel fixings.

Teak

Tectona grandis - 660kg/m³.
From Burma/Thailand
Mid/dark-brown hardwood often with thin, darker brown markings and stripes. Works and carves very well. Not usually available from sustainable sources. Can be oily when first cut causing problems with some finishes. Most suitable surface protection is an oil finish such as teak oil. Wearing a dust mask is recommended when sanding.

Walnut, American Black

Juglans nigra - 660kg/m³.
From North America
Dark brown, almost purple hardwood, as opposed to European walnut which is a mid to dark brown colour with thin black streaks. Used extensively for quality furniture and gun stocks. Both American black and European walnut are very expensive and supplies are often limited.

HOW TO BUY WOOD

Timber merchants themselves buy rough sawn timber, and you too can buy wood in an unplaned state and machine your own. However, you can often have timber prepared to size for you by the sawmill. This advice should help you when ordering.

Wood is most commonly sold in nominal sizes. This means that the size shown describes the size that the mill starts off with and not what the finished dimensions will be. If finished sizes are important, make sure that you specify them – if not, expect the final measurement to be around 3mm (⅛in) to 6mm (¼in) undersize.

When timber is cut to size and planed on all of its surfaces, if these edges are all at 90 degrees to each other, the timber trade describes the timber as PSE – Planed Square Edge, or sometimes PAR – Planed All Round. Where faces may not be at 90 degrees to each other, perhaps where splays or chamfers are being machined too, the description is PAR – Planed All Round.

Timber can also be cut to length. This is known as crosscutting, and this may help with handling and loading. If the finished length is important, order the timber as 'crosscut exact to length'.

After timber has been dried it is unwise to recut it in its thickness, as it will have a tendency to cup.

HOW WOOD CAN MOVE WHEN CUT

Plain sawn (also known as flat sawn)

wood is sliced tangentially to rings

as it shrinks wood cups in direction of rings

boxed heart

appearance of board

Quarter cut (also known as rift sawn)

wood is sliced radially to rings

as it shrinks wood stays relatively flat

appearance of board

HOW WOOD WARPS

bow

spring

cup

twist

Above: Although a wide range of different woods is available, staining increases the choice of colours even further (see page 106 for how to apply wood stains)

MAN-MADE BOARDS

There is nothing quite like real wood, but if expense is a factor, or where there may be problems with the movement of solid wood (see page 9) you may prefer to use man-made sheet materials. These fall into several categories:

Blockboard and Laminboard: Manufactured boards consisting of a thick core of wooden strips held in place by veneers glued to each face. Laminboard has much thinner strips in the core and although similar to blockboard, is much more stable. Suitable for internal use only. Not suitable for areas which may become wet, such as near sinks and baths. MDF has largely superceded blockboard and laminboard for many uses.

Chipboard: Essentially a compressed mulch of wood chippings and glue, which, after being left to dry, cut to size and sanded, produces a relatively cheap sheet material. The quality of chipboard can vary tremendously depending on the size of chippings used, especially in the core of the board. Suitable for internal use only. Often available with coloured or decorative patterned melamine faces to both sides. Extensively used for flat pack furniture, kitchens, fitted furniture and, depending on the density, floors and general joinery.

Fibreboard: Not to be confused with MDF, true fibreboard has natural wood fibres and resins compressed to thickness to make a sheet material. There are three sorts: **soft board**, used for insulation materials and suspended ceiling tiles; **medium board**, used for notice boards; and **hardboard**. Hardboard is a very familiar sheet material. Although most commonly it has a shiny dark brown face, it is also available with patterns or decoration impressed into it. Before using hardboard, soak the back first with water and leave it to dry, to allow it to condition and stabilize to a new environment. Always store flat.

Medium Density Fibreboard (MDF): A fine homogenous board consisting of fine wood particles held together by the use of adhesives. MDF is relatively expensive but as a material it will take veneers, is easily moulded, takes stains and polishes and, unlike chipboard, satisfactorily holds wood screws. It produces very fine dust when worked and suitable precautions should be taken.

Plywood: Manufactured from thin veneers of timber, cross-laminated for extra strength. Plywood usually has an odd number of layers to create a balanced construction. If an even number of veneers is used, there is an increased chance of the board twisting. Plywood is available with decorative timbers bonded to one or both faces and some types are used for external as well as internal work depending on the type of glue used. Marine plywood is the most durable external plywood.

TECHNICAL TALK

BALANCED CONSTRUCTION When one material, for example a veneer, is glued to a baseboard, unless a similar veneer is fastened to the underside too to balance it, the sheet material will cup in a similar way to solid wood

CUP a form of warping (see page 14)

DEAD KNOTS Knots created when branches have been broken off a living tree and wood has grown around them. The dark line around their outside edges is old bark

GRADING Batches of timber divided according to quality

HOMOGENOUS A material of uniform particle size and construction throughout

LIVE KNOTS Knots created by branches that were active when the tree was felled

NOMINAL SIZES The wood sizes with which a sawmill starts before planing: these can vary. Remember that if the sawmill has re-cut timber, the nominal size itself may be smaller than expected.

RING-POROUS Describes hardwoods that have a very definite pattern created by the alternating coarse and fine texture of each ring, e.g. oak and ash

TOOLS

Tools can be expensive, so it is very important to buy right. Always select each tool as you need it rather than all at once – and buy the best you can afford. This way you will build up your tool kit slowly and carefully, adding to it as you get more advanced.

On the following pages, each section is carefully laid out and explains what tools do and how they work, what to look for and what questions to ask. There are shopping guides to help you decide what you need as well as tips and technical talk boxes which cut through the jargon.

If you have a specialist interest, there are many more tools to be found in the full Stanley Tools Catalogue.

MEASURING AND MARKING OUT TOOLS

The whole point of woodwork is to produce straight lengths of wood, to make true and accurate frames and carcases, and to position and fit doors, drawers and shelves. It stands to reason that the instrument you use to do the measuring and marking out should be as precise as possible.

The more accurate the tools you use, the better the chances are of your workmanship looking professional. Always take extra time and care to work exactly to any markings you have made. You should never be tempted in quality woodwork to think 'that's near-enough'! In some instances you may even need to use precision engineering quality measuring and marking out equipment.

It is important to work as accurately as you can because even such apparently small measurements as 1–2mm (⅟₃₂–⅟₁₆in) can easily be seen later. If you need proof, then reach for a rule and look at the actual size that this measures. Now, imagine a gap as large as that on one of your joints!

It can often be very tempting to bypass the careful preparation and accurate marking out of wood, because of your understandable enthusiasm for wanting to make a start on the woodwork itself. But the importance of preparation and marking out really cannot be underestimated. Done poorly, everyone can see the joint that didn't quite make it, or the top that doesn't quite fit. But done well – that's a different story altogether.

The Knife Versus the Pencil

You use a knife to mark on the exact positions of joints. It is much more accurate than a pencil and will actually cut through the fibres of the wood, allowing the saw or chisel to produce a fine, clean edge. Pencils are for marking information on wood – such as face side and face edge symbols (see page 64) – and can be used to show the approximate positions of joints in joinery work.

MARKING OUT SHOULDER LINES

Take extra care marking on shoulder lines. Badly marked out joints are easily spotted after cutting

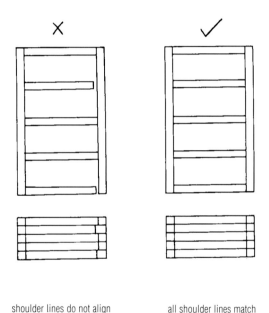

shoulder lines do not align   all shoulder lines match

And make sure that knife lines meet!
(See Marking Out page 64)

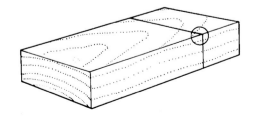

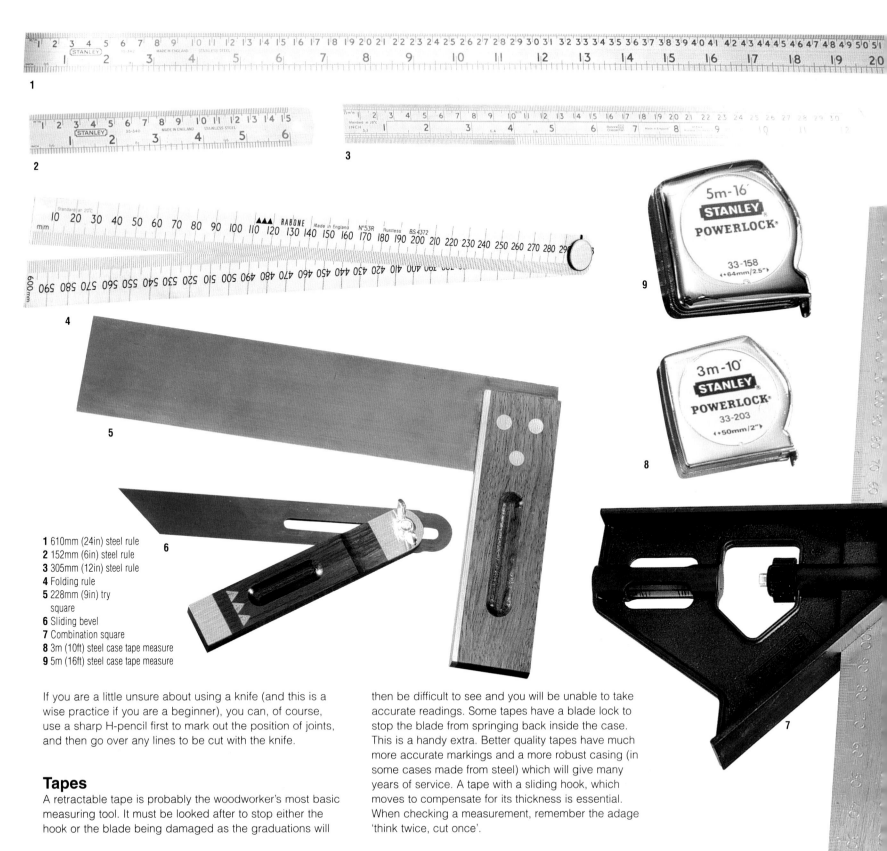

1 610mm (24in) steel rule
2 152mm (6in) steel rule
3 305mm (12in) steel rule
4 Folding rule
5 228mm (9in) try
  square
6 Sliding bevel
7 Combination square
8 3m (10ft) steel case tape measure
9 5m (16ft) steel case tape measure

If you are a little unsure about using a knife (and this is a wise practice if you are a beginner), you can, of course, use a sharp H-pencil first to mark out the position of joints, and then go over any lines to be cut with the knife.

Tapes

A retractable tape is probably the woodworker's most basic measuring tool. It must be looked after to stop either the hook or the blade being damaged as the graduations will then be difficult to see and you will be unable to take accurate readings. Some tapes have a blade lock to stop the blade from springing back inside the case. This is a handy extra. Better quality tapes have much more accurate markings and a more robust casing (in some cases made from steel) which will give many years of service. A tape with a sliding hook, which moves to compensate for its thickness is essential. When checking a measurement, remember the adage 'think twice, cut once'.

19

HOW TO MEASURE EXTERNAL DIMENSIONS

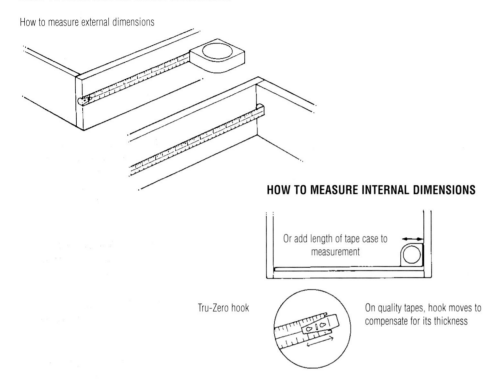

How to measure external dimensions

HOW TO MEASURE INTERNAL DIMENSIONS

Or add length of tape case to measurement

Tru-Zero hook

On quality tapes, hook moves to compensate for its thickness

Steel Rules

Steel rules are more accurate and convenient than tape measures when working on small components, rails and panels. They are especially suitable for measuring the distances between shoulder lines. The graduations usually start right at one end of the rule, enabling it to be pushed into tight corners, and easily allowing you to take a true reading. The most popular sizes are 152mm (6in), 305mm (12in), 610mm (24in) and 1m (39⅜in) lengths. The one metre rule is also known as a metre stick. Steel rules are also very useful for checking the flatness of surfaces during hand planing (see page 70).

Combination Squares

A combination square is a particularly useful tool. For the serious or professional craftsman in fact, it really is a must. Good quality combination squares will allow you accurately to mark out right angles, bevels (see page 74), and mitres. The combination square can also double up as a try square for checking internal angles, or can be used as a separate steel rule. It can even become a depth gauge simply by putting the stock on the surface of the wood and sliding the rule into the hole to check how deep it is.

TRY SQUARE

The try square is used to mark lines across the surface of wood. To use one, put the point of a pencil or knife on the wood in the correct place and then slide the square up to it. The square will automatically stop in the correct position for marking out. Hold the square firmly, pushing down on to the wood. Be careful not to slip when using a knife.

Try squares with a traditional wooden stock are used both for marking out and also for checking the squareness of cabinet work and frames during gluing up (see page 90).

HOW TO TEST A SQUARE FOR BEING SQUARE

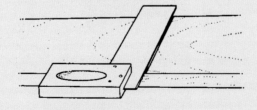

From a true edge mark on a knife line

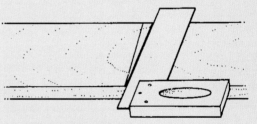

Turn square over to check blade against knife line. An accurate square will line up exactly

Folding Rules

Folding rules are traditionally made from wood, although they are available in plastic and steel too. They are used for the same purposes as a steel rule but fold up to make them much more convenient to carry. For on-site work this also helps stop the rule being accidentally damaged.

Sliding Bevel

A sliding bevel will allow you to set up to a specific angle and then transfer this information exactly to the workpiece. Ensure that when in use, you tighten the adjustment nut or locking lever properly, and do not drop or knock it as this will change the setting. When marking out, do not push excessively against the blade with a marking knife as this too may accidentally alter the angle.

Knives

Knives used for woodwork fall into three categories – marking knives, craft knives and trimming knives.

Marking knives have a flattish wooden handle and, more importantly, the blade has a bevel on only one side. Use the marking knife by putting the face without the bevel against a square or a template, such as another joint – as, for example, when marking out dovetails (see page 86).

Craft knives are much sharper than marking knives and are suitable for cutting materials such as veneers, paper or card. If you use a craft knife as a marking knife you must allow for the width of the bevel on the blade. Be careful with craft knives. Always work so that if you slip, there will be no chance of serious injury.

The typical Stanley trimming knife is a particularly tough knife offering a choice of different shaped blades. These are used where extra precision is required or where you need to work in an awkward space or very tight corner.

Marking and Cutting Gauges

Marking gauges differ from cutting gauges in that the first has a point designed for scribing lines along the grain, while the second has a knife for scoring the fibres of the wood across the grain.

Marking gauges are available with either one point or two (one of which is movable), and used properly they will always give true, accurate gauge lines to work to. A single pointed marking gauge could be used to mark on the depth of halving joints, whereas twin-pointed ones, known as mortise gauges, are used to mark out two parallel lines, for example for mortise and tenon joints.

Cutting gauges are used where it is impractical to use a square and knife across the grain. A cutting gauge will produce a scored line exactly parallel to the end of a board or panel. It is important that the end you use to guide the stock should be true and straight, and that you ensure that the stock is pushed firmly against it to create an accurate line.

THE DIFFERENCE BETWEEN A MARKING KNIFE AND A CRAFT KNIFE

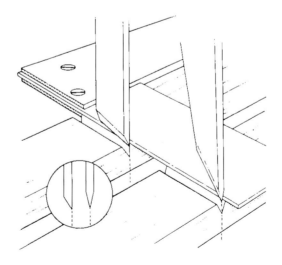

Marking knife blade is only bevelled on one side allowing it to be pushed up to a square

Craft knife has a bevel on both edges creating a "v". This must be allowed for during marking out

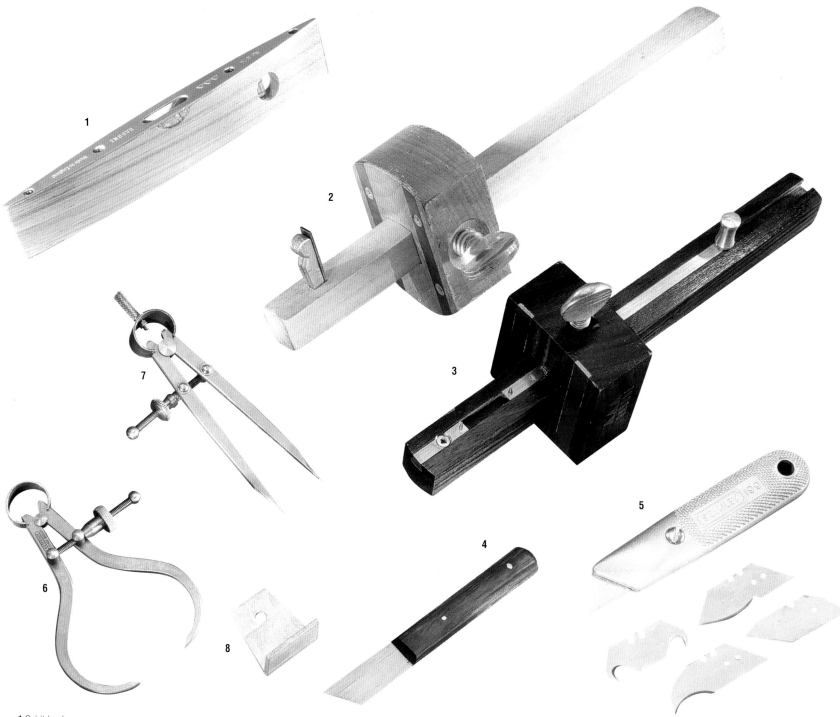

1 Spirit level
2 Cutting gauge
3 Marking gauge
4 Marking knife
5 Stanley trimming knife
   with a selection of blades
6 Callipers
7 Dividers
8 Dovetail gauge

Dividers and Calipers

Dividers are straight-legged and look a little like a pair of compasses with two points. In woodwork, two pairs are used to measure the widths of the pins and tails when marking out dovetail joints. They can also be used to transfer measurements from a surface where using a rule is impractical. Callipers are different from dividers in that they have bowed legs and are used for measuring the external or internal diameters of turned work or other cylindrical objects.

CONVERTING WANEY-EDGED BOARDS

Waney-edged boards can be marked to produce a straight line for sawing by using a chalked line

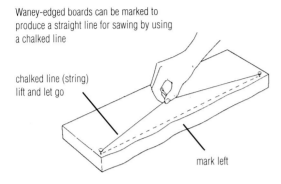

chalked line (string) lift and let go

mark left

Or you can screw or nail a straight piece of wood to the face and push that against the fence of a circular saw

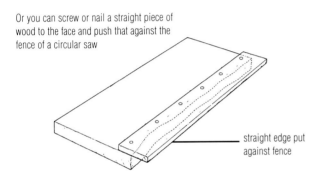

straight edge put against fence

Dovetail Gauge

A small gauge used to mark the angles of dovetail joints. Usually available as either 1:6 or 1:8 angle of slope, the steeper angle (1:6) being more suited to softwoods, and 1:8, hardwoods. You can buy a dovetail gauge or make one yourself by cutting and filing thin metal plate to size.

Spirit Level

Spirit levels are not used in traditional furniture making but are used when installing fitted furniture, including wardrobes and kitchen units. They rely on a trapped air bubble held in a liquid kept in a slightly curved, clear tube. By measuring the position of the bubble, a true horizontal or vertical surface can be found. Modern, top quality box-section spirit levels are virtually unbreakable and have sealed vials.

Other Marking Out Tools

There are several specialist marking out tools readily available, such as profile gauges, trammels and depth gauges. These can be used when an unusual shape or component needs to be marked out.

TIP

A quick approximate gauge line can be achieved by holding a pencil and running the fingers down the edge of the wood

pencil line

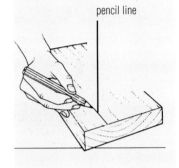

SHOPPING GUIDE

ESSENTIAL TOOLS

TAPE MEASURE 3m (10ft) metal case. The tape must have an accurately marked blade – look for the ⓘⓘ symbol. Blade coating protects against wear

TRY SQUARE 228mm (9in) Should have a hardened and tempered steel blade securely fixed to stock. Other sizes 152mm (6in) and 305mm (12in). Some squares have a 45 degree angle for mitres

STEEL RULE 305mm (12in) Graduations must be accurately and clearly marked

CRAFT/TRIMMING KNIFE Essential for many purposes, including marking out when a marking knife is not available. The blade should be fixed to allow pressure to be applied

MARKING GAUGE Quality varies tremendously. Buy the best you can afford. Must be manufactured for accuracy. Mortise gauges should have a thumb screw to adjust the pins. It is essential that the stock slides smoothly and locks positively in place

SUGGESTED ADDITONAL TOOLS

COMBINATION SQUARE 305mm (12in) Must be accurately manufactured and well made. Check that the rule slides freely and

does not wander

STEEL RULE 152mm (6in) and 1m (39in)

SPIRIT LEVEL Should be precisely machined and have flat working faces. Vials should give accurate readings

DOVETAIL GAUGE If you make your own (see above), ensure that the angles on both sides of the gauge are symmetrical and filed flat

MARKING KNIFE A good quality marking knife is an accurate tool. Safer than a craft or trimming knife

SAWS

Some traditional hand saws are no longer made, but you may have one in a tool box. With the introduction of new materials and manufacturing techniques, the jobs of cutting along and across the grain can now be taken care of by one hand saw, with universal teeth. These cut on the forward stroke; and they are resharpenable.

If you intend to cut sheet materials, be warned that the glue content will rapidly blunt conventional saw teeth, so choose a saw with aggressive geometry fast cut teeth. These cut on the forward and reverse strokes. Saws with these teeth include the Stanley range of Jet Cut saws.

Modern saws are often shorter than traditional patterns. Stubby versions will fit into a tool box making them ideal for quick jobs around the home.

Knowing how to use a saw is of fundamental importance when working in wood – but how do you know which one to choose?

TRADITIONAL SAWS

Hand Saws
Hand saws have a flexible blade to allow you to cut through large sections of wood or across wide panels. The combination of length, toothsize and type of tooth determines the job to which each is best suited.

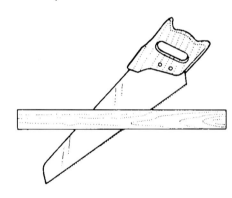

Rip Saw generally no longer manufactured, these are long saws used to cut wood along the grain. Blade length 650mm (26in); PPI 4½–6.

Crosscut Saw used to cut across the grain. Blade length 600–650mm (24–26in); PPI 7–8

Panel Saw similar to a crosscut saw but with finer teeth. Ideal for thin plywood. Blade length 500–550mm (20–22in); PPI 10–12

Back Saws
Back saws have a blade strengthened with either a brass or steel strip. This helps to keep the blade rigid for cutting accurate joints. Back saws are shorter than hand saws and they also have finer teeth.

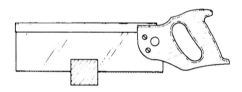

Tenon Saw the most common back saw. Used to cut joints such as the mortise and tenon. Blade length 250–350mm (10–14in); PPI 13–15

Dovetail Saw a fine back saw designed to cut accurate joints such as the dovetail. (See also gentleman's back saw, page 28). Blade length 200mm (8in); PPI 16–22

Bead Saw very fine back saw with a straight handle for cutting delicate mouldings and beads. Blade length 200mm (8in); PPI 26

Hard Point Teeth
Specially hardened teeth, blackened for identification, that stay sharp at least five times longer than conventional teeth. Suitable for cutting sheet materials. Not resharpenable. Disposable and generally less expensive than sharpenable saws

1

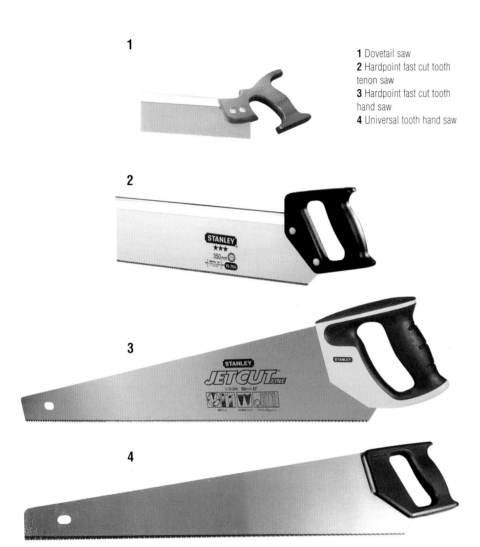

1 Dovetail saw
2 Hardpoint fast cut tooth tenon saw
3 Hardpoint fast cut tooth hand saw
4 Universal tooth hand saw

2

3

4

MEASURING TOOTHSIZE

Saw teeth are measured by points per inch (PPI), or sometimes by teeth per inch (TPI). There is always one less tooth per inch than there are points per inch (e.g. 7 TPI = 8 PPI). The higher the number, the finer the teeth.

QUICK GUIDE TO SIZE AND FUNCTION
Up to 7 PPI   heavy duty sawing and constructional work
8–10 PPI   general purpose sawing
11 PPI and above   fine or accurate work

For the best results, choose the saw with the correct tooth type and size for the job you are doing.

THE CUTTING EDGE

Saw teeth cut the wood, then lift and carry out the waste in the form of sawdust. Different teeth do different jobs

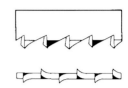

RIP SAW TEETH chisel type teeth that do not score the wood before cutting. Used along the grain only

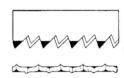

CROSSCUT TEETH knife point teeth that actually sever the fibres of the wood. Ideal for cutting across the grain

FLEAM TEETH also known as straight or needle teeth. Designed for fast cutting across the grain. Especially suitable for softwoods

UNIVERSAL TEETH designed to cut both along and across the grain and found on both hand and back saws

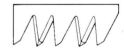

AGGRESSIVE GEOMETRY FAST CUT TEETH produce a very clean quick cut. They cut both on the back and forward strokes. Suitable for cutting modern sheet materials. These are available hardpointed for a longer life

HOW TO USE A SAW

Always saw to an accurate line and cut on the waste side (see marking out, page 64). This will help produce a good clean cut.

How to Use a Back Saw

Use a bench hook and start sawing at a shallow angle. Use the thumb of your left hand as a guide.

Hold the saw in your right hand and start by drawing the saw towards you lightly. Use the thumb of your other hand as a guide, resting it on the wood and up against (not underneath!) the saw blade. Do not let the blade bounce or jump up and down. Now lightly push the saw away from you, and you will start to cut the wood. Use

Below: Use a bench hook and start sawing at a shallow angle. Use the thumb of your left hand as a guide.

only light pressure at first, increasing it slightly as you begin to saw.

Concentrate on following the knife line and do not hold the saw too stiffly. Relax and let the saw follow the line. Aim to saw at an angle of around 15–20 degrees to the wood (a little less when using a dovetail saw), which will allow you to cut into the top corner farthest away from you. After four or five strokes, level out and cut along the knife line on the waste side, working your way through the wood.

Handles and Stance

If you hold a saw properly, the angle of the handle should help you to stand correctly. For example, a dovetail saw handle is set low, allowing you to crouch and 'shoot'

If you make a 'V' with a chisel on the waste side of the knife line, this will help the saw start in the right place

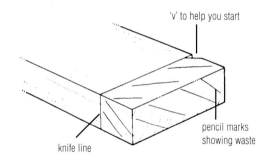

'v' to help you start

pencil marks showing waste

knife line

GOOD ADVICE

Never force a saw blade. If one becomes jammed, find out why. The chances are that you are not sawing straight or true to the line, resulting in the blade becoming trapped in the saw cut (kerf). Relax your arm muscles and resaw to the line. A little paraffin wax (candle wax) on the blade will help the saw blade glide more freely through the wood.

through a dovetail. On the other hand the tenon saw handle will allow you to stand more upright, so you can easily follow your marking out lines.

How to Use a Hand Saw

Hand saws are not intended to be as accurate as back saws. Therefore, when cutting a sheet of plywood or a softwood joist you can work to a clear pencil line instead of a more accurate knife line. If you make an error in marking out, always clearly re-mark your work.

Sawing with a hand saw is similar to sawing with a back saw, the difference being that you start cutting at a slightly higher angle. Do not use a bench hook. Again

draw back the blade using the thumb of your other hand as a guide, and the saw will begin to cut on the forward stroke.

Ensure that the waste is properly supported, especially near the end of sawing. If not, as the waste falls off, the piece you want will also be damaged.

Use the full length of the saw, slightly lowering the angle after two or three strokes. Work with the entire length of your arm, using your shoulder and upper body for power and control. Relax. Let the saw do the work: do not use excessive pressure. Use a little less force at the tip, then slightly increase the pressure as you push forward, until you reach the area of blade near the handle. Draw back and push again. Simple!

SOLVING PROBLEMS

PROBLEM	CAUSE	WHAT TO DO
saw sticks in saw cut (kerf)	> incorrect set on saw > resinous/wet wood > wandering from line during cutting, thus trapping the blade	saw must be reset by a saw doctor use paraffin wax (candle wax) to lubricate blade remove blade and resaw to line
edges break out (splinter)	> toothsize too large for material being cut	select a finer toothed saw
wood tears out from under saw cut, especially when cutting plywood/chipboard	> holding saw at too steep an angle > using excessive pressure	reduce angle of saw to 15–20 degrees use lighter pressure
wood tears out from underneath when cutting across the grain	> as above	fasten a block beneath to support the wood where the grain is tearing out, or on smaller pieces use a bench hook
saw jumps or bounces as you start sawing	> toothsize too large > angle of sawing too steep	select a finer toothed saw reduce angle of saw

SPECIAL SAWS

Sawing isn't always about cutting joints and large pieces of wood; there are other jobs that call for specially designed saws.

Gentleman's Back Saw

The gentleman's back saw can be considered either a dovetail saw or a bead saw, depending on the number of teeth per inch. It is used for finer woodwork, such as cutting and fitting small mouldings and joints in thin hardwood. This type of saw has a straight handle rather than a pistol or closed grip, making it suitable for lighter woodwork. The finer the teeth, the finer the work.

Use the saw as you would a dovetail saw (see how to use a back saw, page 26), pushing it backwards and forwards while keeping it parallel to the bench top. A gentleman's back saw cuts on the forward stroke.

Some gentleman's back saws have an 'offset' handle for cutting through tenons and dowels flush with the surface.

Coping and Fret Saws

In appearance a coping saw is similar to a fret saw, although in fact they both perform very different tasks. The coping saw is the smaller but more heavy duty of the two. It has a replacement blade with 15–17 PPI. It is used to cut around tight curves in softwoods, most hardwoods and in man-made boards up to 25mm (1in) thick. The fret saw has a much taller, deep bowed frame and a very fine blade. Unlike a coping saw it is used to cut extremely light fretwork, and veneers.

A much larger version of the coping saw, which produces only shallow curves in thicker stock, is the traditional wooden framed bow saw. This is quite a heavy saw and is difficult to use, requiring both hands to keep control.

1 Saw and mitre guide
2 Mitre box
3 Gentleman's back saw offset handle
4 Fret saw
5 Gentleman's back saw
6 Coping saw

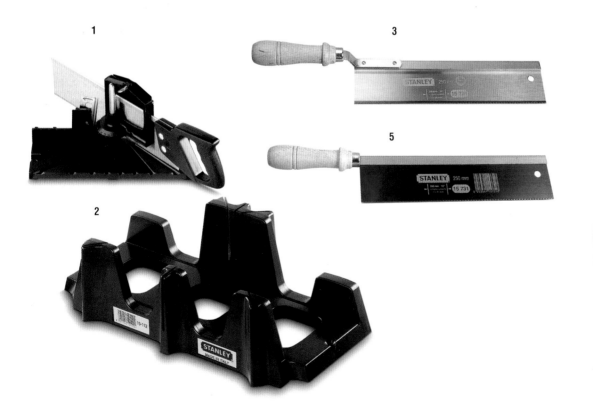
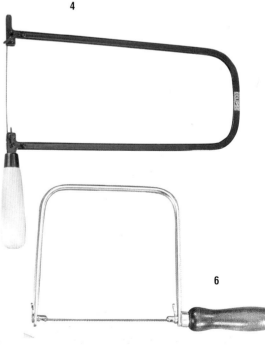

How to Use a Coping Saw

The coping saw can be set up to cut either on the back or on the forward stroke. (The fretsaw, on the other hand, always cuts on the back stroke.) Hold the work upright in a vice and keep the coping saw blade at right angles to the surface of the wood. As with hand and back saws, use the thumb of your left hand as a guide for the blade and use light strokes to help the saw get started. The blade is thin and brittle, so do not force it as you work or it will easily break – instead let the saw do the work. Ensure you do not allow the blade to leave the line you are following. You can help to keep control by turning the blade periodically as you cut. If the wood vibrates in the vice move it nearer to the jaws to stop it juddering.

If you need to start cutting in a totally enclosed area, drill a small pilot hole first (preferably in a corner) and insert the coping saw blade through it, before starting to saw.

Using a Fret Saw

Fret saws cut on the pull stroke and are used only on thin material e.g. veneers. If the overhang is excessive and the wood begins to vibrate, you can make a 'v'-shaped supporting block for underneath to hold and control the wood

USING A FRET SAW

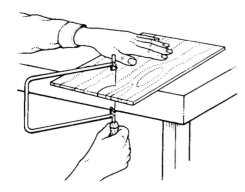

Right: Holding the coping saw with both hands will give you more control. If the material being sawn judders or vibrates, lower it as near to the vice jaws as possible.

Cutting Angles – The Mitre Box

A simple mitre box is a tool to allow you to cut angles at 45 degrees, useful when you need to produce a right-angled joint, for example, on panels and picture frames. It will usually cut at 90 degrees too, for cutting wood to length. More complex mitre boxes can be set to cut at 30 degrees, 45 degrees, 60 degrees, 90 degrees and other angles. They can be bought complete with a back saw, which is held in place by guides. These are more expensive than the simple mitre box but are able to produce very accurate joints.

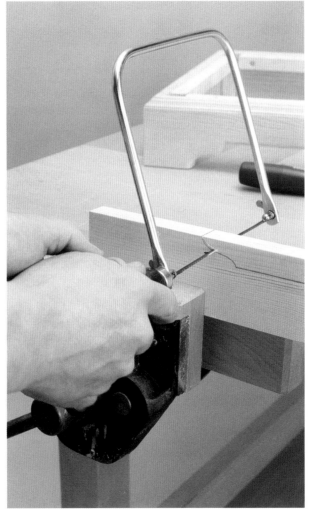

ESSENTIAL TOOLS

500–550mm (20–22IN) HAND SAW (8 PPI) Used for straight saw cuts or for preliminary cutting of timber to length. By selecting a saw with either universal or aggressive geometry fast cut teeth timber can be cut either along or across the grain

250mm (10IN) TENON SAW Used to cut joints and to perform other accurate saw cuts. It is essential that the saw you buy feels both comfortable and well-balanced

SUGGESTED ADDITIONAL TOOLS

160mm (6⅜IN) COPING SAW For cutting tight curves and other shapes

DOVETAIL SAW For cutting very fine joints especially in hardwoods. A good quality traditional pattern dovetail saw usually has a closed grip handle made of wood

TIP

When mitring lots of very small mouldings or beads at 45 degrees you can use the reflection of the beading in the saw blade to give you a quick and simple guide to 90 degrees.

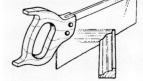

PLANES

Planes are used to make wood smooth, and there are several to choose from. Each is sharpened and set to perform different jobs.

Think of a wood shaving as roughly the same thickness as a sheet of paper. Now hold just six pages of this book between your fingers and imagine a gap this wide on a furniture joint: you can see that it is important to learn how to use each kind of plane, without taking off too much wood.

Planes can either be referred to by name or by a series of numbers. See pages 58 and 59 for further information on how to sharpen the blade.

Note the try plane, jack plane and fore plane are all sharpened and honed so that the plane blade is convex (see page 59).

1 Smoothing plane
2 Jointer or try plane
3 Fore plane
4 Jack plane
5 Block plane

Jack Plane

There are two basic sizes – the No.5 (50mm (2in) wide blade) and the No.5½ (60mm (2⅜in) wide blade). The primary functions of a jack plane are to remove excess wood, and to smooth and flatten rough-sawn or distorted wood (see page 70). Before you use a jack plane, the wood should be dry and secondary conditioned (see page 10). A jack plane is a medium-length plane – 355–380mm (14–15in) – meaning that it is light enough to work with for long periods of time, yet still long enough to level out bumps. See page 70 for the correct method of using a jack plane.

Try Plane or Jointer Plane

The basic size is the No.7 (60mm (2⅜in) wide blade). A try plane is longer than a jack plane – 560mm (22in) – and is used to make long edges straight; to correct edges that are out of square; and for the edge jointing of boards (see page

79). If sharpened and set up properly, the edge that the try plane produces can be adjusted and made true, independent of any adjacent faces (see page 73). If you are careful, you can work to very fine tolerances, and take off just one shaving at a time to produce a perfect edge joint.

Fore Plane

The basic size is the No.6 (60mm (2⅜in) wide blade). The fore plane is longer than the jack plane but shorter than the try plane – 460mm (18in) – and thus is an ideal in-between plane, able to perform the jobs of both the other planes. The fore plane can be sharpened and set in different ways, according to the type of work.

Smoothing Plane

The sizes are the No.3 (45mm (1¾in) wide blade), No.4 50mm (2in) wide blade), and No.4½ (60mm (2⅜in) wide blade). A smoothing plane is used for cleaning up and to flatten out any ridges left by the jack, fore or try planes. The end of the blade is sharpened so that it is straight rather than convex, with its two corners slightly rounded off to stop the edges of the blade digging into the wood. The set on a good smoothing plane can be altered from coarse to extremely fine by using the frog adjustment (see right). When working, plane the surface following the direction of grain rather than from one end of a piece of wood to the other. This could mean working at an angle across the surface of the wood, or using a slicing, circular motion (for the technique see page 94).

Block Plane

The sizes are the No.60½ (with a low-angle blade of 13½ degrees) and the No.9½ (with a blade angle of 21 degrees). Block planes are small hand planes, with a blade held at a very shallow angle (bevel uppermost). They are used to plane small components, including composite sheet materials, and specifically the end grain of solid wood. Block planes have only a single iron (plane blade), rather than a double iron (plane blade and cap iron) as in the case of most bench planes.

THE PARTS OF A BENCH PLANE

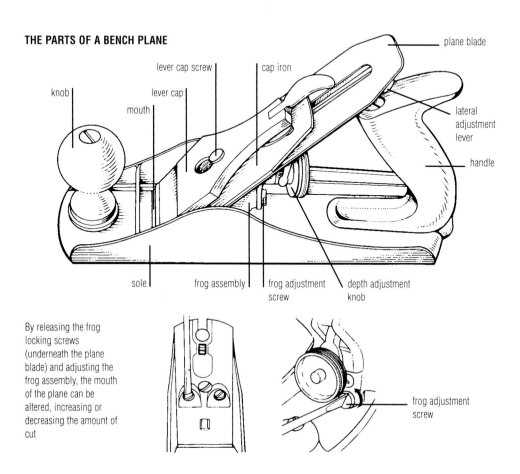

By releasing the frog locking screws (underneath the plane blade) and adjusting the frog assembly, the mouth of the plane can be altered, increasing or decreasing the amount of cut

frog adjustment screw

HOW TO SET A PLANE

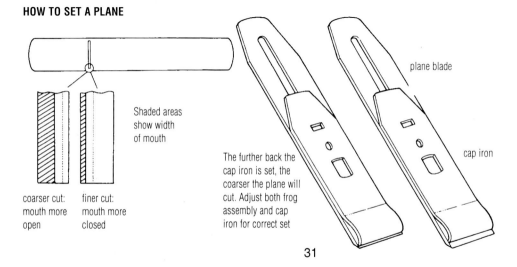

Shaded areas show width of mouth

coarser cut: mouth more open

finer cut: mouth more closed

The further back the cap iron is set, the coarser the plane will cut. Adjust both frog assembly and cap iron for correct set

plane blade

cap iron

31

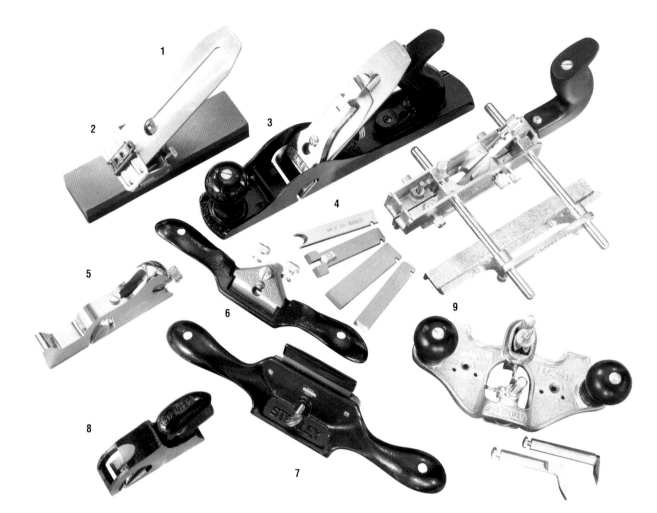

1 Bench plane blade
2 Honing guide
3 Bench rebate plane
4 Combination/plough plane
5 Cabinet makers' shoulder plane
6 Spokeshave
7 Scraper plane
8 Cabinet makers' bullnose plane
9 Router plane

SPECIAL PLANES

As with most tools, some planes have been developed to perform special tasks. Here are just a few . . .

Rebate Plane

A bench rebate plane has a mouth which extends across the entire width of the sole of the plane. This enables a rebate (sometimes called a rabbet) to be worked, usually along the grain from one end of a piece of wood to the other. Rebate planes vary in length from 235mm (9 $\frac{1}{4}$in) to 330mm (13in). Some have a knife (cutting spur) to score the fibres of the wood, ready for working across the grain as well as along it. To help keep the rebate size accurate, some rebate planes have adjustable depth and fence gauges. These are known as fillister planes.

Shoulder Plane

Shoulder planes are smaller than rebate planes and have a shallow cutting angle for working across the grain. They do not usually have depth and fence gauges as they are used for the cleaning up of shoulders of joints, especially when fitting wide tenons and housing joints. Some shoulder planes have removable fronts to convert them into a 'chisel plane', which can be used to work into the corner of a stopped rebate. A variation on the shoulder plane is the bullnose plane, which is shorter and has a much smaller sole in front of the actual cutting edge.

Plough Plane and Combination Plane

Largely superceded by the electric router, a plough plane cuts grooves, whereas a combination plane combines the jobs of both rebate and plough planes. It may also have extra profile cutters for producing beadings or for tongue and groove work.

Scraper Plane

This is sometimes called a cabinet scraper although, being strictly accurate, a true scraper is a piece of tool steel with burred-over edges. The scraper plane performs the same function as the traditional hand cabinet scraper – i.e. it removes torn grain – but its rigid body does not give the same flexibility and control. However, scraper planes are

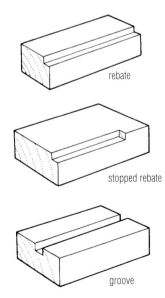

rebate

stopped rebate

groove

HOW TO ADJUST A WOODEN PLANE

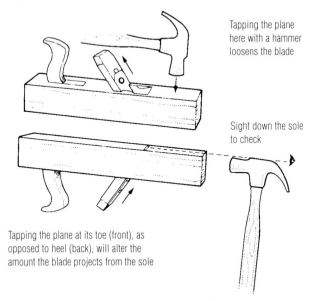

Tapping the plane here with a hammer loosens the blade

Sight down the sole to check

Tapping the plane at its toe (front), as opposed to heel (back), will alter the amount the blade projects from the sole

generally easier to work with, and on surfaces that are to be heavily scraped there is no risk of fatigue (hand cabinet scrapers may well make your thumbs sore and can even cause blisters). See page 34.

Router Plane

Router planes have a blade set below the sole, which allows the plane to fit comfortably into a trench. They are especially handy for cleaning out the long trenches which run across a grain in traditional through and stopped housing joints.

PUSHING A SPOKE SHAVE AWAY FROM THE BODY

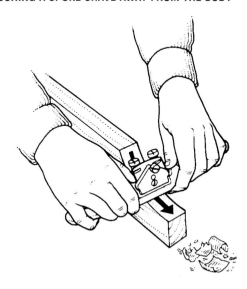

Spoke Shave

There are two main sorts of spoke shave. The first is a flat-based (or straight-faced) spoke shave, which is used to smooth convex edges. The second is the round-based (or round-faced) spoke shave, which will clean up and prepare concave edges. There is a special skill to using spoke shaves, which takes time to practise: this is the reason why in inexperienced hands they have a tendency to judder along the surface of the wood (usually caused by the blade protruding too far from the sole). It is common to push a spoke shave away from you during use, although some craftsmen prefer to use it on the pull stroke.

TIP

Although the blade of a bench plane may give years of good service, at some point in time you may need to order a new one. The following information should help you.

The standard length of a bench plane blade is usually 185 mm (7¼in), but the width varies depending on the type of plane. These are usually 45mm (1¾in), 50mm (2in), 55mm (2⅛in) or 60mm (2⅜in) and when ordering blades, this size must be specified. It is also wise to tell the tool shop the model/product number of the plane.

HONING GUIDE

Mastering the skills of sharpening plane blades and chisels can take time and lots of practice. The skills are not difficult to learn but it can be frustrating when the final cutting edge is not how you intended it to be! Honing guides hold the blade being sharpened at a steady angle, which takes away the guesswork and allows you to concentrate on pushing the blade backwards and forwards. The only disadvantage to using a guide is that because the wheel actually runs on the stone, in effect this reduces the length of it. You must therefore be careful not to let the stone become hollow or uneven during sharpening. For the technique of honing, see page 58.

A honing guide will help steady a blade during sharpening

The Cabinet Scraper

When hand planing, even with a sharp, finely set blade, it is still possible to pull out the fibres of the wood. This produces torn grain, which is a direct result of the fibres running through a board in many different directions. Fortunately, this defect can easily be rectified by the use of a cabinet scraper. It is important to learn the proper techniques of preparing, using, and sharpening a scraper or you could very well create more problems than those produced by the bench planes in the first place.

HOW TO USE A SCRAPER

When you use a jack plane, the convex plane blade creates small ridges running along the surface of the wood. The smoothing plane removes these marks, but may tear up the grain slightly as it does so. A cabinet scraper will remove this defect.

Never scrape along the length of the wood. This will create more small ridges on the wood which are very difficult to sand out. Instead, scrape the wood at constantly varying angles to the edges of the wood. Do not scrape directly across or along the grain.

Hold the scraper with both hands in a relaxed manner, using your thumbs to flex it (see photograph below). The more you bend the scraper, the more it cuts.

Hold it at an angle between 30 degrees and 45 degrees to the surface of the wood, although the exact angle will depend on the burr produced during sharpening. The lower the angle at which you hold the scraper, the more it cuts. Beware of holding it too low, because it will dig in. The angle and the degree to which you flex the scraper, determine together the total amount of cut as you work.

After scraping the surface, it is preferable to sand the wood along the grain by hand, using 80/100 grit garnet paper. Work through the grades carefully using finer and finer papers as you progress (see page 98).

1 Scraper plane
2 Cabinet scraper
3 Goose-neck cabinet scraper

PREPARING A SCRAPER FOR SHARPENING

1 First of all, put the scraper in a vice with one of the long flat edges uppermost. Take a medium/fine file and use it to file from one end of the scraper to the other. This will keep the edge square and flat.

2 Next, draw-file lightly along the edge of the scraper to remove any coarse file marks. Turn the cabinet scraper over and prepare the second long edge as above.

3 On the top of an oil stone remove the four 'burrs' that have been produced (one long edge has two sides). Keep the side of the scraper flat against the stone and use firm pressure, pushing backwards and forwards.

4 Put the lid on the oil stone box and, using this as a jig, push the scraper against the side of the stone to prepare two polished, square edges. Clean any excess oil from the scraper.

HOW TO USE A TICKETER TO SHARPEN A SCRAPER

A ticketer is also known as a burnisher. The technique of sharpening a scraper requires practice.

1 Hold the cabinet scraper, resting one of the short edges in the palm of your left hand, and have the other short edge pushing against a bench top. Flex the scraper slightly with your thumb.

2 Hold the ticketer at around 70 degrees to the front face of the scraper and draw it firmly towards you along the side to be sharpened, starting from near the bottom. Push the ticketer against the scraper with an action similar to that of sharpening a knife with a steel. Do not use a steel or screwdriver to sharpen a scraper.

3 Repeat this process for the back of the scraper but this time push away from you at an angle of 70 degrees, again from near the bottom.

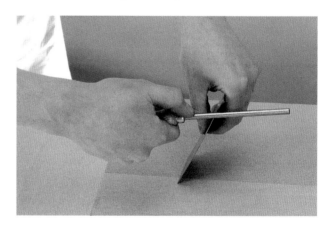

4 Next, turn the scraper right over so that the other short end rests on the bench, and burr over the front and then the back, as before. This will result in two strokes in total being delivered at the centre. Repeat this process to sharpen both sides of the other long edge of the scraper. This produces four sharp cutting edges in total.

THE STANLEY SURFORM

The Surform is a specially designed tool for rasping, trimming and filing curved and compound shapes. Surforms do not take the place of good quality bench planes; instead they have about 450 teeth on a standard-cut 255mm (10in) blade, which cut away at the wood like miniature chisels. Surforms do not need sharpening or adjusting during use. The Stanley Surform is a safe and

versatile tool and does not require any special skill to use. It is especially suitable for shaping and smoothing unusual patterns and mouldings.

The Surform is available both as a metal-bodied tool, or in strong plastic (glass reinforced polypropylene). There are many different varieties of Surform, suitable for a wide range of job applications.

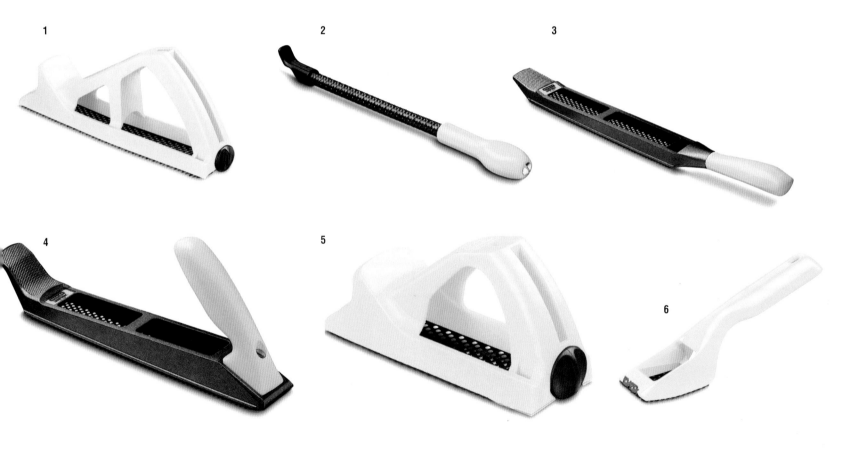

1 Surform moulded body plane
2 Surform round file
3 Surform flat file
4 Surform metal body plane and file
5 Surform moulded body block plane
6 Surform moulded body shaver tool

TECHNICAL TALK

CAP IRON Breaks off wood shavings pushing them clear of the mouth. It is important that it sits flush on the plane blade or the mouth will quickly become blocked

REBATE A recess along the edge of a piece of wood. Also known as a rabbet

TONGUE AND GROOVE A type of edge joint between two boards that allows for shrinkage. A tongue on one piece fits into a groove on the other. Most often found on wooden floor boarding

TRENCH A groove which runs across the width of a piece of wood

Surform Specifications

Metal body

	Surforms o/a length	Length of blade
Planer file	310mm (12½in)	250mm (9¾in)
Plane	315mm (12½in)	250mm (9¾in)
Flat file	440mm (17¼in)	250mm (9¾in)
Block plane	155mm (6¼in)	140mm (5½in)
Round file	365mm (14¼in)	250mm (9¾in)

Moulded body
thumb screw for blade release

Flat file	300mm (11¾in)	140 (5½in)
Plane	270mm (10½in)	250 (9¾in)
Block plane	155mm (6¼in)	140 (5½in)
Shaver tool	185mm (7¼in)	64 (2½in)

SHOPPING GUIDE

Note all plane bodies should be cast iron and precision ground for flatness and squareness. Controls should be easy to adjust and plane blades should be made from good quality tool steel.

ESSENTIAL TOOLS

NO 4 SMOOTHING PLANE For general purpose work, cleaning up and smoothing

NO 5½ JACK PLANE For general roughing down of timber and rapid stock removal

SUGGESTED ADDITIONAL TOOLS

NO 7 JOINTER/TRY PLANE For the accurate squaring up of long edges

NO 60½ BLOCK PLANE For accurate cleaning up of end grain

SURFORM BLADE TYPES FOR DIFFERENT DEGREES OF FINISH

standard

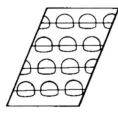
half round

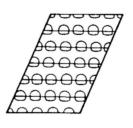
fine

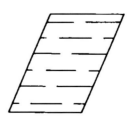
metal/plastic

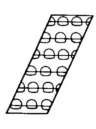
round

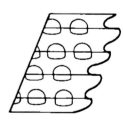
curved

HAMMERS AND MALLETS

There is more to hammers and mallets than the apparent simplicity of knocking in a nail might lead us to believe.

Hammers

A well made and properly used hammer will last for many years. A hammer should have a comfortable, well balanced, shock-resistant handle, and the striking face of the head should be hardened – after all, it stands to reason that a hammer should be harder than the object it's hitting.

When using a hammer, always deliver a fair blow. The face of the hammer should hit the object, whether a nail or a wooden block, square on. Select the correct hammer type and weight for the job (see page 41) and make sure you do not accidentally damage or hit the handle when you are performing heavier duty tasks.

(see page 41)

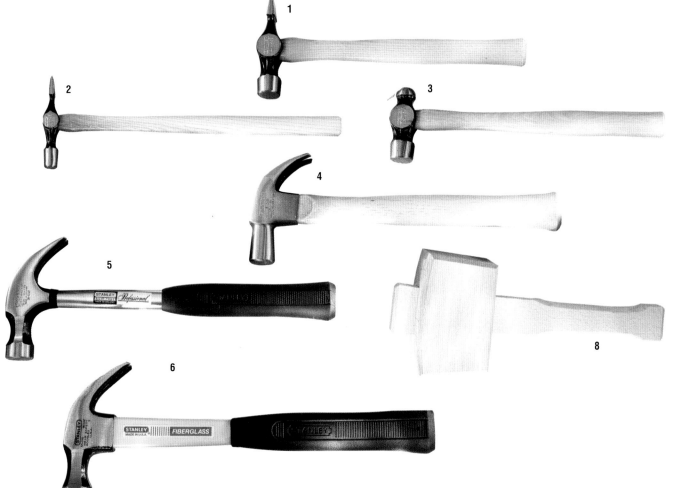

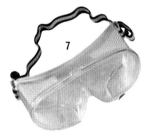

1 Cross-pein (Warrington) hammer
2 Pin or telephone hammer
3 Ball-pein hammer
4 Wooden handled claw hammer
5 Steel handled claw hammer
6 Fibre glass handled claw hammer
7 Safety goggles
8 Carpenter's mallet

SAFETY

Safe working practices are essential when using hammers and mallets. Thumbs and other parts of the human body are rather easy to flatten! Ensure that the hammer head is not loose and that the handle is not damaged, worn or split. A hammer with a badly worn head should be discarded. Dirty hammer heads can easily be cleaned by using emery cloth; put the emery cloth on the workbench and, using a circular motion, move the hammer head around on it, pressing firmly but carefully. The wearing of eye protectors is highly recommended when using a hammer.

CLAW

weight	365g (13oz); 450g (16oz); 570g (20oz); 680g (24oz)
use	general purpose joinery; insertion and removal of nails
look for	head – forged, polished, heat-treated steel; handle – tubular steel or wooden, well-secured to head

PIN

weight	100g (3½oz); 115g (4oz)
use	light duty work including driving in of panel pins and veneer pins
look for	head – see claw hammers; handle – see cross-pein hammers

BALL-PEIN

weight	various from 115g–1360g (4–48oz)
use	engineering
look for	head and handle – see claw hammers

CROSS-PEIN (WARRINGTON)

weight	170g (6oz); 225g (8oz); 280g (10oz); 340g (12oz); 400g (14oz); 450g (16oz)
use	cabinet work and top quality joinery; driving some nails and pins into awkward areas
look for	head – see claw hammers; handle – wooden (ash or hickory) for shock absorption

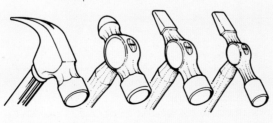

claw hammer   ball-pein   cross-pein   pin hammer
                (engineer's)   (Warrington)
                hammer   hammer

Hammer Types

Through the generations, dozens of hammer types have been developed. Some are very specialized and the layman could have fun guessing what they could be used for; others are far more familiar.

The Handle

The important considerations for the hammer handle are comfort, strength and the fixing of the head.

Steel handles should be made from tubular steel, driven into the head under pressure.

Wooden handles, made from hickory or ash, are selected for their straight grain. The handles should be fixed with either double or triple wedges. Smaller hammers – under 225g (8oz) – may have one hornbeam wedge and one of malleable iron.

USE A HAMMER AND BLOCK TO SEPARATE JOINTS

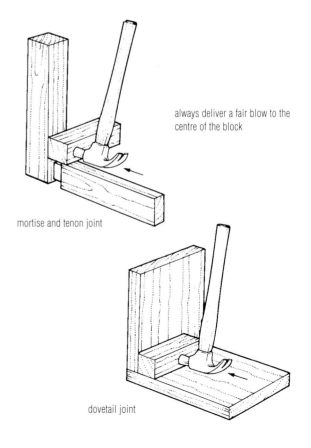

always deliver a fair blow to the centre of the block

mortise and tenon joint

dovetail joint

WHICH NAIL?

ROUND WIRE A strong nail made from round-section steel for construction work

OVAL WIRE General purpose nail made from oval-section wire. Designed to reduce the chance of wood splitting

LOST HEAD Round-section nail with a small head allowing it to be punched below the surface

PANEL PIN Used to fasten thin plywood or hardboard, or to secure small joints and mouldings. Veneer pins are even thinner and are used to hold veneers in place

DOVETAIL NAILING
Also called cross or skew nailing. If you insert nails into a joint at alternating angles so the nails grip the grain, a stronger joint is produced than by straight nailing

REMOVING NAILS
Always protect the surface with a block, or with thin plywood or card, when using pincers or a claw hammer to remove nails

Mallets

The mallets used in woodwork are usually made of wood themselves, and unlike hammers, they never have a steel head. The reason for this is simple – mallets are specifically designed to be used with tools, offering them protection but still allowing complete control. In order to increase their weight, carpenter's mallets (used to chop out joints) have a large head and are often made from beech, a timber which is close grained, quite hard and very resistant to impact.

HOW TO USE A CARPENTER'S MALLET

For chopping out mortises, use a controlled clean stroke. Do not lift the mallet much more than 300mm (12in) from the chisel handle between blows – if you strike from any higher than this, you will lose control. Use the face of the mallet for most work, although you can use the side of the mallet head (or the palm of your hand) to tap the chisel gently during the cleaning up of joints.

Good Habits

Do not use a mallet to knock joints apart, as its square corners will damage the work and the flat face will spread the blow – use a hammer.

For the greatest control, always strike a chisel with the centre of the mallet face, never near its edges.

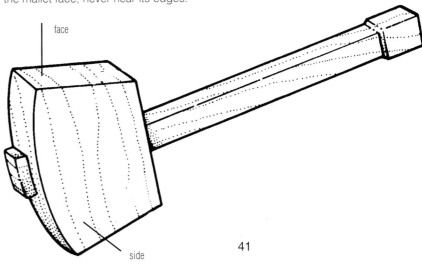

face

side

41

CHISELS

There are three basic types of chisel. These are firmer chisels, bevel-edged/paring chisels, and mortise chisels. Each was originally designed to perform distinctly different tasks.

TRADITIONAL CHISELS

Firmer Chisels

Traditionally made with square edges to the blade, which provides extra strength for work such as chopping out joints. As this usually means being hit with a mallet, they are of strong construction. The handle, usually wooden, has a ferrule where the blade tang enters the handle and may be strengthened at the top to stop it splitting.

Bevel-Edged Chisels

More slender than firmer chisels, having the edges of the blade chamfered off, allowing the chisel to be worked into corners, and thus especially useful for cleaning up joints. These chisels were originally not intended to be hit with a mallet, and the wooden handle was not usually strengthened. A paring chisel is a specific type of bevel-edged chisel, being longer and more slender still, giving the craftsman extra control to work back to a line, accurately pushing with the weight of the upper body. With a well sharpened chisel, this body weight would usually be sufficient to cut through the wood cleanly.

1 Firmer chisel
2 Bevel edge chisel
3 Bevel edge paring chisel
4 Carver handle
5 Oval, moulded handle

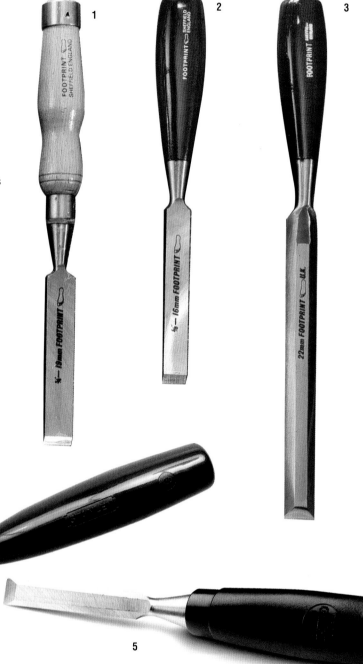

Mortise Chisels

Much stronger than the other types, mortise chisels have a thicker blade that is long and tapered so that it can be pulled on to remove waste while cutting out deep mortises.

All three basic types of chisel are still available today, some made to original patterns, depending on the manufacturer. But with the development of new materials there have been changes too. Handles are now often made from polypropylene, a plastic of immense strength. Some woodworkers still prefer the feel of wooden handles, but plastic handles are certainly much stronger and more resistant to impact.

Modern steel bevel-edged chisels can often perform the tasks of both the traditional firmer and bevel-edged chisels. Chisels such as the Stanley 5002 series, for example, can safely be used for heavy duty jobs as well as much more delicate work. However, if you are ever in any doubt about a particular range, always refer to individual manufacturer's instructions.

Handle Types

There are three main types of chisel handle.
Always try out the feel of the handle before you buy: a good chisel should feel comfortable and well-balanced.

Carver The traditional style of handle for bevel-edged and paring chisels. Available in either wood or plastic

Octagonal Usually wooden but not quite as comfortable to use as the carver handle. Designed to stop the chisel rolling off the workbench

Oval The oval section stops the chisel rolling around on the workbench. A heavier duty pattern than the carver handle

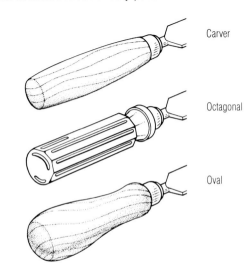

Carver

Octagonal

Oval

WHAT MAKES A GOOD CHISEL?

FEATURE	WHAT TO LOOK FOR
Top quality steel blade hardened and tempered, flat ground faces	Chisel blades should be capable of achieving a keen edge during sharpening. The strength and reliability of the steel are critical. Stanley chisels are made from chrome alloy, a steel similar to that used in the manufacture of ball bearings
Balance	A chisel should feel well balanced and comfortable, becoming in effect an extension of your hand
Handle	The handle should feel comfortable and be capable of withstanding blows with a mallet
Secure handle fixing	It is important that the handle cannot twist or work loose during use. On the Stanley 5002 series the bolster and tang are friction-welded together. Even under destructive testing where the blade is bent to 45 degrees, the weld should still not fail

HOW TO USE A CHISEL

Chisels are designed to cut or chop away at wood and to do this they are either struck with a mallet or pushed into the wood. For example, when cutting deep mortises, a mallet will provide extra force, whereas when cleaning up or working back to a line (paring), the weight of your body will usually be enough.

Vertical Paring

Vertical paring means working from above and pushing the chisel down, on to and through the wood, to remove a corner or small edge, or to work back to a marking line.

1 First fasten the workpiece to a bench with a G-clamp (make sure you put a scrap of wood on top of and underneath the workpiece as protection) – see page 55.

2 Sandwich the chisel blade (about 38mm (1½in) from the end) in your left hand between your thumb and your index finger, with your thumb at the back

3 Put your middle finger just below your index finger at the back of the chisel, below your thumb. The chisel should rest against the middle third of your middle finger.

4 Use these two fingers and your thumb to hold the chisel firmly, for proper control. You can use your ring finger in addition to your middle finger for extra power.

5 Rest your left hand on top of the workpiece with the chisel edge above the part to be pared off. Position your little finger slightly behind the others for comfort. Do not

attempt to take off too much wood at once and carefully work back to a knife line.

6 Next, lean over the chisel with your body so that your right shoulder is over the chisel handle. Hold the chisel handle firmly in your right hand.

7 Either use just your right hand to push down on the chisel, or for extra force gently use the weight of your shoulder, pushing against your right hand to pare off the waste.

Horizontal Paring

Horizontal paring is performed when you are cleaning out the bottom of joints, such as the halving joint (see opposite). It is always best to hold the workpiece steady in a vice.

1 Put the joint to be cleaned up into the vice just above the marking gauge line to which you are working.

2 Let the chisel blade rest (bevel edge up) across all four fingers of your left hand (palm uppermost), lying roughly against the bottom third of your fingers. Your left hand gives the control. Hold the chisel in place with your thumb about half-way down.

3 Either push the chisel into the wood using the pad of your right hand against the handle (perhaps lightly tapping the chisel with this fleshy part of your hand), or firmly grip the handle with your right hand and push toward the wood. The aim is gently to push or strike the chisel handle, carefully cutting into the wood.

VERTICAL PARING

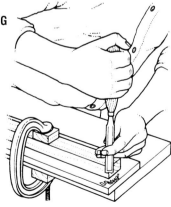

HORIZONTAL PARING

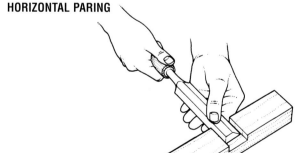

Left: Do not work all the way across the joint from one edge to the other or the fibres will tear out on the back edge. Instead, work just past half-way through and turn the piece of wood around so that you cut from both edges. Ensure that the bottom of the joint is quite flat by gently cleaning up with a chisel

HOW TO USE A MALLET AND MORTISE CHISEL TO CUT A MORTISE

Always secure the work firmly (see page 55). It is important that the workpiece is not allowed to slip while you are using a mallet and chisel. Protect the bench with a chopping board and use G-clamps (also known as G-cramps) to hold the work in place.

Hold the chisel upright in your left hand with the bevel edge facing away from you. Wrap all your fingers around the chisel handle with your knuckles facing away from you. Hold the chisel firmly but relax your grip slightly for comfort.

Standing behind or just to one side of the workpiece, hold the mallet in your right hand and deliver a firm blow to the

chisel handle. Do not use a hammer! Always keep the chisel perfectly upright and at 90 degrees to the surface of the wood (test with a square if necessary). After the first blow move the chisel back slightly and strike the chisel again. Any waste from the second blow will be left in the hole produced by the first strike. Remove this as you go by pulling back on the chisel.

Start from the centre of the mortise, working in one direction towards you. After a few strikes turn the chisel around completely so that the bevel is facing you and remove the other half of the mortise by working away from you.

Make sure you leave a small amount of waste at both ends of the mortise for cleaning up. See page 39 for more details on hammers and mallets, and page 82 for more on removing waste.

SHOPPING GUIDE

ESSENTIAL TOOLS

BEVEL EDGE CHISELS: 6mm (¼in); 12mm (½in); 18mm (¾in); 25mm (1in). Essential for cutting and cleaning up joints in basic woodwork

SUGGESTED ADDITIONAL TOOLS

BEVEL EDGE CHISELS: 4mm (⅛in); 10mm (⅜in); 16mm (⅝in). The first is not available in the Stanley 5002 range

MORTISE CHISEL: 6mm (¼in)

HAND DRILLS AND BRACES

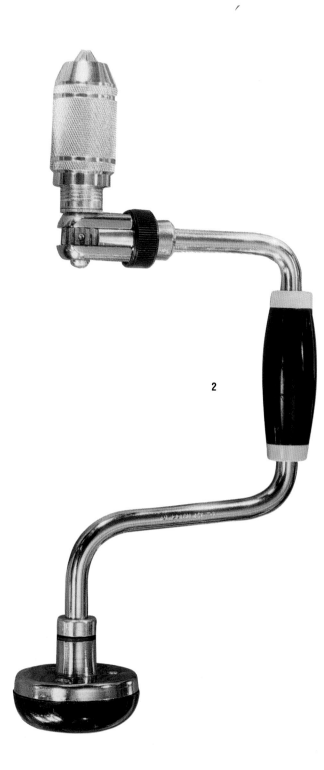

There are two basic hand tools which, in conjunction with a variety of drill bits, bore holes in wood. These are known as either a hand drill or a brace.

The brace is a larger and more heavy-duty tool than the hand drill. It is intended to be used with larger drill bits such as centre bits, augers and expansive bits for the drilling of large-diameter or deep holes. The much faster rotating hand drill is used with smaller twist drill bits.

At the business end of each tool is a chuck which tightens on to the drill bit, holding it firm and allowing it to bite into the wood without slipping. Note that each chuck is designed to accept only a certain type of bit (see page 48). The chuck can develop quite a grip on the bit during use; if you follow the procedure described opposite you will be able to remove the bit more easily after use.

When to Use a Hand Drill
The hand drill has gearing to increase its chuck speed and permit fast boring of small holes. It is only suitable for straight shank drill bits (twist drills) and for some 'special' drill bits, including counter sink bits. Hand drills are most often used to drill pilot and clearance holes for wood screws.

When to Use a Brace
A brace works slowly, one revolution of the handle being one turn of the chuck. The cranked handle offers a lot of leverage and the brace is built to drill deep, wide holes, slowly and accurately. Some braces have ratchet attachments that will allow you to work up against a cabinet side or wall. Expansive bits will allow you to bore a wide range of large-diameter holes but they are less robust than a centre bit.

1 Hand drill
2 Ratchet brace

46

HOW TO INSERT AND REMOVE DRILL BITS

Hand Drill

To remove drill bits, hold the hand drill chuck firmly in your left hand. Clasp the drive handle in your right. Turn it towards you in an anti-clockwise direction. By suddenly stopping the chuck turning, you will release the drill bit. You may find it helpful to steady the hand drill against your body which will give extra pulling power. To insert a drill bit, do the same operation in reverse.

Brace

The method is essentially the same as for the hand drill above. Hold the chuck in your left hand and, steadying the brace against your body, turn the cranked handle anti-clockwise, by pulling towards you. Use firm pressure. If you do this in reverse it will tighten the chuck.

THE SIMPLEST BORERS OF WOOD

Bradawl

A very simple tool, essentially a length of round wire flattened at one end and fastened into a handle. It is used to make starter holes for drilling and inserting screws. Place the flattened end across the fibres of the wood to break them and twist the tool while pushing to open up the hole.

Gimlet

A particularly useful tool, having a drill bit with a screw tip. The screw helps to pull the gimlet into the wood while the drill clears out waste from the hole. It is able to produce deeper and more accurate starter holes than a bradawl.

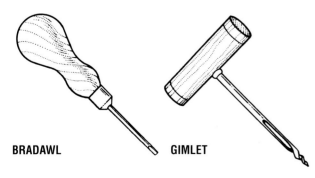

BRADAWL   **GIMLET**

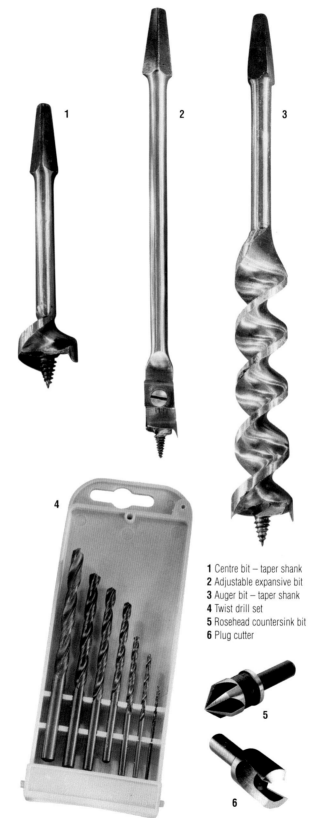

1 Centre bit – taper shank
2 Adjustable expansive bit
3 Auger bit – taper shank
4 Twist drill set
5 Rosehead countersink bit
6 Plug cutter

JAWS

The design of the jaws of a chuck guarantees that they grip a drill bit to stop it turning. Jaws will hold only certain types of drill bit and here is a guide to which ones do what.

UNIVERSAL JAWS Some jaw types, known as universal jaws, are able to hold No 1 morse taper bits, straight shank (twist drills) as well as the more usual auger bits. In case of doubt, refer to the manufacturer's instructions.

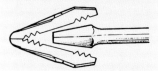

ALLIGATOR JAWS The jaws of most braces are designed to hold only square taper shank auger bits and will not accept or grip on to other sorts of drill bit.

HOW TO USE A HAND DRILL

Always stay in control by clamping the workpiece to the bench or holding it steady in a vice. A sharp drill bit will easily cut through wood without any excessive pushing. When drilling small holes, hold the hand drill with the drive handle in your right hand and use your left hand to hold the steadying handle (the one at the opposite end of the drill from the chuck). You may need to use a little extra pressure from your body but do not overdo this. Use a square or some other guide, if necessary, to ensure that you are working at the correct angle to the surface.

Before starting to drill, mark the exact position of the hole on the wood with a sharp steel pointer. This will stop the bit from wandering across the surface of the wood as you start turning the drive handle. If you prefer to make the pin-point a little larger, turn the drive handle carefully backwards for a quarter to half of a turn, before starting to drill forwards in the normal way. This will enlarge the pin-point and help you start. Always turn the drill slowly to begin with, only gathering speed as the bit begins to bite.

The third handle provides extra pushing power when drilling deeper holes, though do not push too hard, as this will reduce the amount of control you have. If you put a small amount of paraffin wax on the drill bit it will help with boring through resinous wood.

If you are drilling all the way through a piece of wood, it is important not to let the back of the work splinter out. To stop this, position a packing piece firmly behind the wood.

To help remove the drill bit from the wood after drilling, move your left hand (after drilling) to the third handle (opposite the drive handle). This will stop the hand drill spinning and allow you to pull the drill from the wood. Continue turning the drive handle clockwise while backing out from the drill hole.

HOW TO USE A BRACE

The brace is most often used with an auger bit, which has a screw end to position it exactly and to help pull the bit into the wood. The knives (blades) around the end of the bit actually score the wood as it turns, and the waste in-between the screw and these blades is scooped out by the rest of the drill bit. A sharper auger will slowly cut a deep, wide, accurate hole in both softwoods and hardwoods. Mark the starting position with a pointer and start to drill by allowing the screw thread to bite into the wood at this point. Hold the wood to be drilled in a vice, as near to the jaws as possible, as this will provide extra rigidity. Use firm body pressure to help push the drill bit through the wood as you turn the cranked handle clockwise.

Before going all the way through the workpiece, keep checking to see when the screw thread on the drill bit just becomes visible on the other side. At this point, remove the drill by turning it anti-clockwise. Turn the workpiece around in the vice. Drill into the same hole again, this time through the exit hole left by the auger screw. Never push so hard against the brace that you lose control. Let the drill bit do the work.

Right: Use a square to help guide the hand drill.

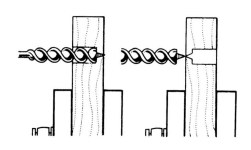

When using a brace and auger bit, drill into the front face until the screw is just visible at the back ...

... then turn the wood around and drill from the back into the exit hole left by the auger screw

PELLETS

Use pellets when a screw-head or hole is to be hidden by the use of a wooden plug.

A pellet cutter produces a small cylindrical piece of timber with the grain running across the face. This is different to a dowel, where the grain runs along its length and provides strength. Pellets are easy to make.

Use a pellet cutter to drill into a scrap piece of wood. It will automatically stop at a certain depth. Next, simply break off the pellet with a screwdriver.

To bore the hole into which the pellet will fit (counterboring):

- Use a twist drill bit of the same diameter as the pellet to bore a wider hole into the clearance hole, see page 53.

- Or, better still, use an auger bit of the same diameter as the pellet, letting the point of the auger mark the exact position where you will drill the pilot and clearance holes later.

Insert the screw into its counterbored hole, tap the pellet into place and clean off with a hand plane. You can use a little glue to hold the pellet in position. Ensure that its figure and colour match the surrounding wood.

DON'T DRILL TOO DEEP

If you accidentally drill too deep, before putting in the screw, mix a stiff paste of fine wood dust and PVA adhesive and squeeze it well into the hole before inserting the wood screw. As the glue dries, the screw will be held securely.

Drilling too far altogether, and allowing the drill bit to pop through the other side of the workpiece is rather more of a problem – none too attractive on a table top! Any gadget to help prevent this has got to be good: the illustrations here give some ideas.

The simplest method is to mark the drill bit indicating where you need to stop; either wrap masking tape around it or paint on paper correction fluid at the appropriate point. The disadvantage is that as the tape or correction

fluid wears off, if you are not very careful, you can actually find yourself drilling deeper and deeper as you progress from one hole to another.

Alternatively, if you have a twist drill, you can use a drill stop. This looks a little like a large washer, which you fasten on the drill bit by means of a small grub screw. Beware, however – if the drill stop touches the workpiece while spinning, it will damage it. Overcome this by using a thin piece of plywood or card, with a hole drilled in it, to protect the wood surface.

A drill block, a square piece of wood with a protruding arm (used as a handle) on one side to stop it spinning around, will both protect the wood and determine how far you drill by its thickness. There is absolutely no risk of damage but making the block can be fiddly and time-consuming.

1 Wrap tape or mark the drill bit with paper correction fluid at the correct depth

2 A drill stop will determine how far to drill but take care not to damage the surface of the wood

3 A drill block is safe to use and will determine how deep you drill according to its thickness

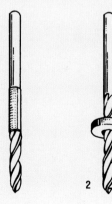

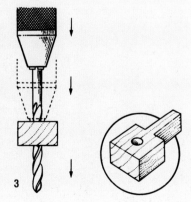

1   2   3

SCREWDRIVERS

Screwdrivers are probably the most misused hand tool in every day use. The problem is that being 'handy', they can be used as a chisel (but to less effect) and they are perfect, are they not, as steel wedges for pulling two bits of wood apart and or taking off paint tin lids!

I was once fitting some doors on a cabinet in our workshop, when a gas fitter working on the building asked me whether I had a large screwdriver he could borrow. If I had not asked him how large he actually meant I would not have discovered he simply wanted it to knock a brick off a wall …

The real truth of the matter is that if you use a screwdriver for anything other than driving in screws you will almost inevitably cause irreparable damage to it.If you want to produce quality woodwork, make sure you always look after your screwdrivers properly and they will go on working perfectly for years.

TRADITIONAL SCREWDRIVERS

Logically, the story of the screwdriver starts with that of the screw. Early wood screws were made by hand and were relatively crude affairs, easily identified by their flattened tips. Screws were no longer made by hand after around 1850, when mass-produced screws with fine machined pointed tips began to appear. As engineering standards improved generally, so did the tools used to drive screws into wood.

The essence of the screwdriver is this. A round or square bar is flattened at one end into a blade that fits a slot in the screw. Simple. The bar is hardened and tempered for strength. Top quality screwdrivers have forged tips, precision ground to fit manufactured screws exactly. Then they may be polished, to improve their appearance. Some screwdrivers are left like this; others are finished in a clear lacquer to prevent corrosion.

DO'S AND DONT'S

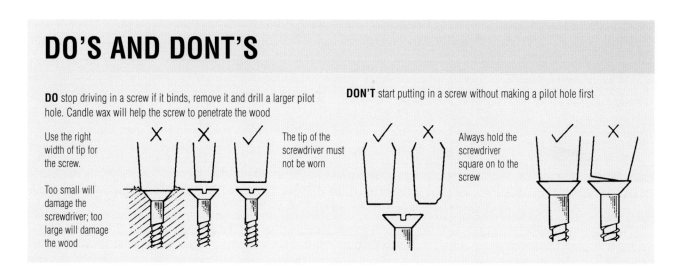

DO stop driving in a screw if it binds, remove it and drill a larger pilot hole. Candle wax will help the screw to penetrate the wood

DON'T start putting in a screw without making a pilot hole first

Use the right width of tip for the screw.

Too small will damage the screwdriver; too large will damage the wood

The tip of the screwdriver must not be worn

Always hold the screwdriver square on to the screw

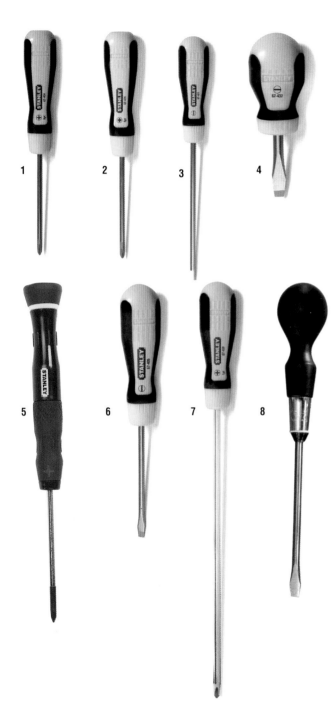

There are two types of screwdriver tip, the first being the slotted type just described, and the second is a more modern invention, the Phillips or crosspoint. This tip is specially designed to prevent the screwdriver slipping and damaging the work.

Handles

Screwdriver handles are often made from injection-moulded polypropylene, rather than wood. This guarantees that the handle is virtually unbreakable and allows the bar to fit securely into the handle. Plastic has not yet entirely superseded wood, however; wooden-handled cabinet screwdrivers are still made and many professional woodworkers prefer the 'feel' of wood. Wooden-handled screwdrivers are generally made from round bar (see right), the handle being fastened in place using a traditional bolster construction process.

OTHER SCREWDRIVERS

There is often a need to put screws into awkward or tight places. Here are some you could choose:

Stubby

Very short, often available with a chunky handle to give good leverage in very tight spaces.

Long Reach

Made extra long so that you can work in an otherwise restricted part of a construction.

Cranked (Offset)

Set at 90 degrees so that you can reach very confined areas. Invaluable at times!

Precision Head

This type of screwdriver is not often used for woodwork but it is available in a range of extremely small tip sizes. They are particularly ideal for clock, watch and spectacle repairs. The end of the handle rotates and fits into the palm of your hand allowing you to turn the screwdriver with your fingers.

BARS AND TIPS

The bar and tip of a screwdriver determine the type of job to which it is best suited

ROUND BAR Generally more suited to working in wood

SQUARE BAR Not generally used for woodwork. Made from square-section steel. A spanner can be used with it to give extra leverage

FLARED TIP Usually forged and then precision ground, providing much more strength than a parallel tip

PARALLEL TIP Usually produced in conjunction with round bar and intended to be used for lighter work, including electronics

CROSSPOINT See Technical Talk, page 52

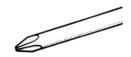

1 Phillips screwdriver
2 Pozidriv screwdriver
3 Parallel tip screwdriver
4 Stubby screwdriver
5 Instrument screwdriver
6 Flared tip screwdriver
7 Long reach screwdriver
8 Wooden cabinet handle screwdriver

POZIDRIV SCREWDRIVER

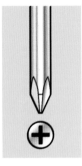

PHILLIPS SCREWDRIVER

SCREWS

Screws are used to fasten one material to another. The type to use depends on the thread of the screw, the head, the materials being joined and the screw size. Some screws look more attractive than others and you may want to consider this too.

All these factors will determine which screw is the best one to use for any particular job. For example, if you are making top quality original or reproduction furniture, the best choice would be steel or brass, slotted, countersunk, wood screws. If all the slots are made to point in the same direction, this can look even more stylish. On the other hand, you may be working in chipboard, where both the material and aesthetic concerns are different. In this case it might be wiser to use a crosspoint screw with a twin thread which is designed for fastening sheet materials. It sounds complicated, but you will understand more as we look at the various types.

Head Shape and Type

Raised Head Generally used to fasten handles and fittings to woodwork. The hole must be countersunk as with flat-headed screws.

Countersunk or Flat Head The traditional wood screw head. The clearance hole will need to be countersunk (using a countersunk bit – see page 47), letting the top of the screw sit flush with or slightly below the surface of the wood.

Round Head The shoulder of the screw lies flush with the surface of the fitting. Often used to secure ironmongery or furniture hardware when impractical to use countersink heads.

Slotted Head Has a simple slot across the screw head, into which the blade of the screwdriver fits.

Crosspoint Head Designed to prevent slipping and therefore damage of the workpiece. Crosspoint heads will not withstand the same amount of leverage as slotted ones. Sometimes the head is adapted slightly to permit the use of both slotted and crosspoint screwdrivers. There are several well known crosspoint head brand names.

The Thread

Traditional Wood Screw Used to fasten softwoods, hardwoods and plywoods, especially in traditional cabinet work and general woodwork.

Twin Thread Very keen pulling power. Especially suitable for fastening man-made sheet materials as the grip is much stronger than a traditional wood screw.

SCREWDRIVERS

Screw size		Size of screwdriver	
gauge no	screw width (mm)	tip to be used tip width for slotted screws (mm)	cross point size
2	2.0	3.5	1
4	2.5	4.0	1
6	3.0	5.0	2
6	3.5	5.5	2
8	4.5	6.5	2
10	5.5	8.0	2
12	5.5	8.0	3

Traditional wood screw

Twin thread wood screw

HOW TO PUT IN A WOOD SCREW

By following a few simple procedures you can guarantee that any pieces of wood you screw together end up exactly where you need them.

First select the size and type of wood screw you need (see page 52) and mark on the wood exactly where the screw holes should be. Use a marking gauge and try square to put a small cross in the correct position. You should use either a sharp pencil or a knife to make the cross.

Next, drill a small pilot hole through both pieces of wood to be joined, going in slightly less than the full length of the screw. Clamp the pieces together to hold them in place if necessary. This pilot hole should be slightly less than the thread size of the screw and will allow the screw to bite into the wood without splitting it. Softwoods, such as pine, usually need a slightly smaller pilot hole than tough hardwoods such as oak.

You now have a hole marking the screw's corresponding position on each piece of wood. Select a second drill bit, either the same size as the gauge of the screw or very slightly larger, and drill through the top piece of wood only. This is called the clearance hole allowing the screw to fit through it.

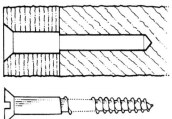

Clearance hole allows screw to pass through one of the pieces of wood

Pilot hole allows screw to bite into wood without splitting it

A sign of quality – flared tip of a screwdriver showing shot-blasting to tip

If the hole needs countersinking use a countersink bit next, but again be careful not to drill too deeply. Now drive in the wood screw, and you will find that the two pieces of wood will be held perfectly in place.

Brass Screws

Brass is very soft, so where brass screws are to be used on cabinet work it is essential that after you have drilled the pilot and clearance holes, you drive a steel screw of the same size and gauge into the screw hole first, and then remove it. If you do this, there is much less chance when you fit the brass screw of it becoming damaged or breaking off at the screw head. Never attempt to force a brass screw into place. I repeat, brass is very soft!

WHAT SCREWS ARE MADE FROM

STEEL	The typical grey wood screw. Suitable for internal use, and external use if protected from moisture which causes rust.
BRASS	Brass screws are very decorative and are essential for use in woods where tannic acid is present, such as oak. They are very soft and must be used with extreme care or the heads will be damaged and may break off. Before driving brass screws home, always pre-drill and screw with steel screws first.
JAPANNED	Black enamelled screws often used for japanned hinges and fittings. Can be used externally.
	Screws can also be chromium-plated, electro-brassed, nickel-plated or made from stainless steel. In case of doubt as to their functions, please consult your supplier.

TOOLS USED FOR HOLDING

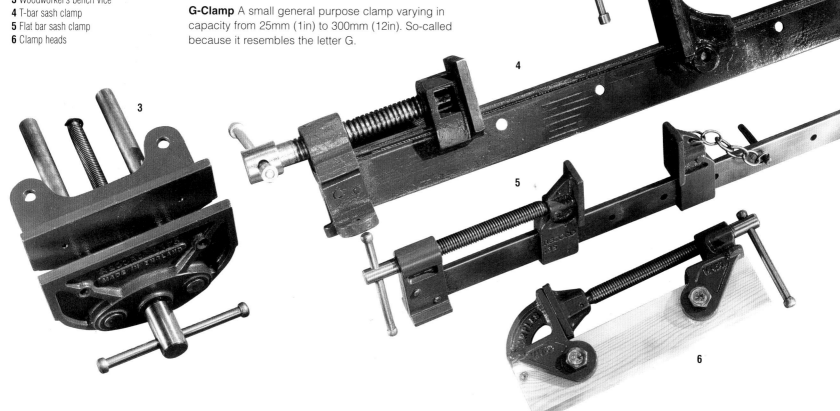

When you are working with wood, there are two main reasons for holding it steady. The first is to allow maximum control during cutting; the second, to keep the wood in position while gluing up. There are several tools for holding wood.

HOW TO USE CLAMPS

Short Clamps
These are used to hold smaller pieces of work or to steady them while cutting. There are several types:

Bench Holdfast Used to hold wood when cutting out joints. Fits through a previously drilled hole in the workbench top.

G-Clamp A small general purpose clamp varying in capacity from 25mm (1in) to 300mm (12in). So-called because it resembles the letter G.

1 Fast action clamp
2 G-clamp
3 Woodworker's bench vice
4 T-bar sash clamp
5 Flat bar sash clamp
6 Clamp heads

F-Clamp Also known as a fast action clamp or speed clamp, this is similar to a G-clamp, but slides more easily to length before being screwed up tight, making adjustments much faster than with a G-clamp. So-called because it resembles the letter F.

Specialized Clamps There is a multitude of unusual clamps – mitre clamps, flooring clamps, edge clamps, quick grip clamps … One thing is for sure, you should be able to find something that will do the job!

Long Clamps

Long clamps are used for gluing up frames, tops and carcase constructions.

Sash Clamps Essentially a long steel bar with a tail slide at one end and a movable head at the other. They are used in the gluing up of frames and carcases. The sash clamp is a simple concept, and an invaluable tool.

The best quality sash clamps are known as T-bar clamps, so-named because they have a T-shaped steel bar, for extra strength. They do not bend when tightened and are heavy clamps to handle.

The flat bar type of sash clamp is suited to much lighter work and is the most usual one for home woodworking. You can use extension pieces to increase the length of both T-bar and flat bar sash clamps.

Another option is to buy separate clamp heads for which you supply your own piece of wood for the bar. With these you decide yourself what the length of the clamp will be. Either beech or maple is suitable for the bar.

There is also available a much longer version of the short F-clamp, which allows for very quick setting up while gluing.

There is more information on page 92 on using sash clamps and keeping frames square.

PROTECT THE WORKPIECE

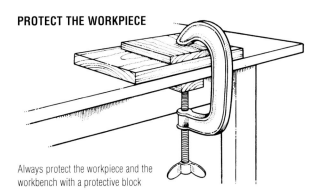

Always protect the workpiece and the workbench with a protective block

KEEPING IT SQUARE

sash clamp and frame being glued

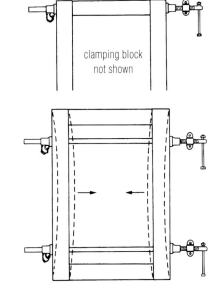

clamping block not shown

Position clamp to align with centre of joint – if not the frame will distort as more pressure is applied

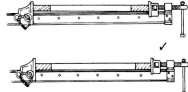

Keep frame flat on sash clamps or use packing pieces of even thickness underneath – even a slight gap will cause problems.

TECHNICAL TALK

CAULS A length of wood curved on one face only and used in conjunction with a pair of G-clamps, which will deliver firm pressure to the centre of a board, pushing it flat

HEAD & TAIL SLIDE The head of a sash clamp is fastened to an adjustable screw thread, whereas the tail slide moves freely along the bar and is secured by means of a steel pin. The tail slide is set to a suitable length for the job before the head of the clamp is tightened

THE VICE

The two single most important tools used in woodwork are the bench and the vice. There are two main sorts of vice: the engineer's vice, which has steel jaws, but stands above the bench top, making it unsuitable for woodwork; and the woodworker's vice. A woodworker's vice had wooden protective pieces which you attach to the jaws to stop the workpiece being damaged. The jaws lie flat and in line with the bench top, allowing you to work, unrestricted, on frames and panels.

The quality of the vice is very important. Always ensure it is well made. It is convenient to have a quick-release mechanism, which allows you to open the jaws to their maximum capacity quickly and easily. It also enables you to close the vice without having to wind it in laboriously.

One word of warning – a vice is designed for holding objects firmly in its jaws, so that you can mark out and cut joints. It is not designed to have whatever it is holding hit with a hammer. This will either damage the screw mechanism or dislodge the fixing screws holding the vice to the bench. Vices are an expensive one-off purchase; if you buy the right one, it will be money well spent, but do not treat it badly.

HOW TO FIT A WOODWORKER'S VICE

1 Fit the wooden jaws to the vice first. The jaws should be made from a dense hardwood, such as beech or maple, and should be between 15mm (⅝in) and 20mm (¾in) thick. Ensure the tops of the jaws are planed flat and level.

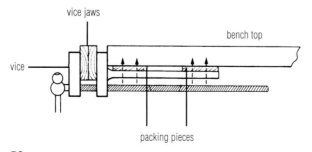

2 Turn the bench upside down on a flat surface and rest the vice (also upside down) on the same surface. This will show you the thickness of the packing pieces you require.

3 Insert the packing pieces. Mark and drill the pilot and clearance holes for fixing the screws. Use large gauge woodworking screws, or coach bolts to fit the vice.

4 Next turn the bench the correct way up. Make sure that the jaws are level with the bench top. Use either a hand plane or make small adjustments to the packing pieces if necessary.

Cabinet Maker's Wooden Bench Vice

Unlike the woodworker's vice (shown) which generally stands proud of the front of the bench and is made for the main part of metal, the cabinet maker's bench vice is a wooden vice having the edge of the bench top as one of its jaws, the other jaw pulling up against it. The advantage is that you are able to hold pieces of wood parallel and right up to the edge of the bench. The disadvantage is that as one of the jaws is actually the bench top, if it becomes damaged, the repair will be very difficult and expensive.

BENCH STOP

A bench stop is a small square block of wood (the stop) fitted to a metal slide which is fastened underneath the bench. This allows it to be raised or lowered through a square hole in the bench top.

Why Use One?

Sometimes woodworkers will try to plane wood to size in a vice. This has two major disadvantages:

• When planing wider boards, a vice is often not wide enough to take the wood, or distorts it as the vice is wound in.

• When planing lengths of wood longer than the vice jaws the ends are unsupported. It is impossible in this situation to make wood flat with a hand plane as its weight will cause the wood to bend.

Web clamp

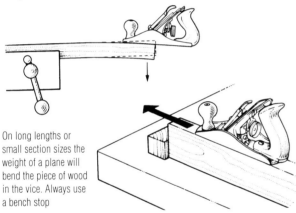

On long lengths or small section sizes the weight of a plane will bend the piece of wood in the vice. Always use a bench stop

the first place, or, if you do, a jig or extra clamp is available to put pressure exactly where you need it. It could easily take you longer to make the jig than perform the task of gluing up!

If the work you are doing involves a particularly awkward shape, such as gluing up a chair, you will usually find there is a special clamp or tool made for the job. If you need to put extra pressure at one specific point, you can easily rig up a quick clamp yourself, such as a loop of string with a stick threaded through to tighten it.

Holding Mitred Frames

There are many ways of holding mitred frames together, some involving quite sophisticated clamps. One of the easiest methods is to use a frame or web clamp. These are ideal for small to medium frames.

1 Cut the mitres and make sure that each pair of lengths making up the frame is exactly the same by putting the pieces back-to-back. Clean up the joints.

2 When gluing up, set the clamp to approximately the right size. Put three of the sides of the frame into the clamp so that inserting the fourth side of the frame puts a slight stress on the clamp. This will gently hold the frame in position. Tighten the clamp fully. It is important to keep the frame flat on a base board and only gently push the fourth side into place.

3 After tightening the clamp, check for square and adjust if necessary.

The second point is the most important one and many woodworkers blame themselves for not being able to produce straight edges. The problem is exacerbated when planing small dimensions. In this case it is essential to use the bench as a supporting flat base, planing up against a bench stop. A vice should only be used to hold pieces such as table tops when planing edges.

HOLDING AWKWARD SHAPES

If you watch a skilled craftsman working, you soon realize that to do a job properly they need special tools. This rule also applies to holding and gluing awkward shapes. The only way to achieve a professional result is to think ahead, which means designing and assembling your project so that either you do not have any awkward shapes to hold in

CARING FOR YOUR TOOL KIT

SHARPENING

The best plane or chisel in the world is useless without a keen cutting edge. Plane blades should, in fact, be so sharp that you could cut human hair with them. An old workshop test was actually to shave hair from the lower forearm with a plane blade. The best ways of improving the quality of your woodwork are to concentrate on the techniques of accurately marking out, to prepare fine cutting edges on your tools and to practise the techniques until you get them right. You cannot only half-sharpen tools and expect them to work correctly – they won't!

Sharpening Plane Blades

When a plane blade is made it is hardened and ground by the manufacturer. The final cutting edge is produced by you, not by the factory. When you acquire the blade, it may not be absolutely flat. Therefore it will need to be 'backed off' on a sharpening stone.

The cutting edge of the blade is formed by honing (sharpening) at a slightly steeper angle than the grinding angle (usually 25 degrees).The best angle at which to hone is approximately 30 degrees. This figure is really an ideal, and as long as you do not make the honing angle too steep or too shallow, you will still be able to achieve a good fine edge. If you are not confident about holding the blade at the correct angle, you may prefer to use a honing guide which will hold the blade steady for you (see page 33).

HOW TO SHARPEN

I use an oil stone to sharpen plane blades and chisels. Put a little light machine oil on the surface of the stone and spread it around with your finger. To produce the cutting edge itself, back off the blade to flatten it, and then hone the front bevel. Backing off the blade will allow the cap iron of the plane to lie perfectly flat on it.

Sharpening a plane blade (backing off)

Honing a plane blade

GRINDING ANGLE

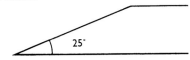

angle at which the blade has been ground at the factory ready for sharpening

HONING ANGLE

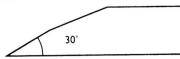

slightly more than the grinding angle, this is the actual cutting edge of a blade

Backing Off

Put the back of the plane blade on the oil stone and push it backwards and forwards using firm pressure. Always keep the blade totally flat against the surface. When it has been backed off completely you will have flattened the full width of the blade at its cutting edge. The steel should appear bright and shiny.

Honing

The next stage is to sharpen the bevel of the plane blade. Put the bevel on the stone's surface and feel where it actually 'sits' on the stone. Then lift the blade up slightly (about 5 degrees) to produce the honing angle. Move the blade backwards and forwards covering the whole surface of the stone (especially the ends of it, which will help to keep the stone flatter). Do not allow the blade to rock as you move it around. The honed edge will soon be seen as a thin, shiny (polished) line at the cutting edge of the blade.

WHAT NEXT?

Keep sharpening until you have backed off the blade and honed it too. Alternate between the two as this makes the process rather less boring! A fine 'wire edge' should form at the cutting edge to indicate that you are nearly there. It should take 20 to 30 minutes to sharpen a new blade, but much less for one that has previously been backed off and honed. After the honing process the blade can be stropped to produce an even keener cutting edge (see page 60).

HOW TO SHARPEN THE PLANE BLADE

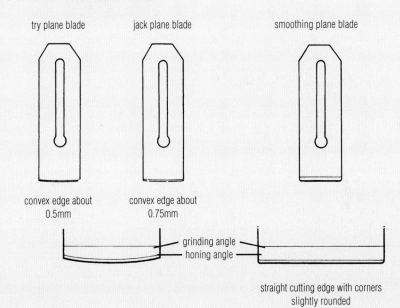

try plane blade   jack plane blade   smoothing plane blade

convex edge about 0.5mm   convex edge about 0.75mm

grinding angle
honing angle

straight cutting edge with corners slightly rounded

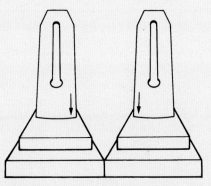

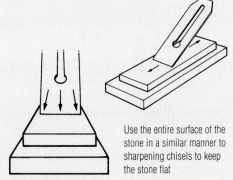

Put pressure on one side then the other to wear the edges more than the centre. Do not try to round the blade by lifting it

Use uniform pressure across the width of a smoothing plane blade

Use the entire surface of the stone in a similar manner to sharpening chisels to keep the stone flat

CONVEX EDGE Jack, try and fore planes have a convex cutting edge put on their blades rather than a straight one. To produce a convex edge, simply put more pressure on the outside edges of the blade as you sharpen it. This wears it more on the edges, to form a slightly rounded edge. Do not try to lift the blade or to round it deliberately as the corners will dig in and damage the stone.

STRAIGHT EDGE If you are sharpening a smoothing plane blade with a straight cutting edge, keep the pressure uniform across both the blade and sharpening stone (ensure that the stone is flat). The corners can be slightly rounded later by lightly stroking them against the edge of the sharpening stone. This will stop the plane blade digging into the surface of the wood during use.

1 Use figure-of-eight movements, circles or long ovals to hone the edge of the chisel. Cover the entire surface of the sharpening stone to keep it flat

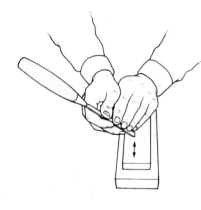

2 Narrow chisels can be controlled by pushing them backwards and forwards at 90 degrees to the edge. Steady the blade by using the side of the stone as a guide

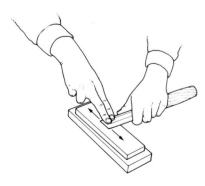

3 Backing off a chisel blade

SHARPENING CHISELS

The rules for sharpening plane blades apply to chisels too. You will have to back off and hone the chisel on a sharpening stone, ensuring that the cutting edge remains uniformly flat and checking that you do not rock the blade as you push it backwards and forwards.

When sharpening a very narrow blade 6mm (¼in) or less there is a great risk that the chisel will wobble from side to side. The best technique is to sharpen it by positioning the chisel at right angles to the stone (see below). Use the side of the stone as a guide for your hands, pushing the chisel backwards and forwards along the stone, but be careful not to remove the skin from your fingers as you work!

Wider chisels can be sharpened by moving the chisel along the length of the stone in long ovals, circles or figure-of-eight movements. Always keep the chisel at the correct angle and never concentrate on just one particular area of the stone as it will wear unevenly.

When the wire edge appears, as with plane blades, you are well on the way to achieving a good cutting edge. If you achieve a wire edge and the chisel will not cut correctly, the chisel is either made from a steel which is not hard enough to sharpen or you are honing the blade at too high an angle.

After honing, strop the blade on a leather, using firm pressure (see below). Always pull the chisel towards you to protect the strop from damage. It is a good idea to use one strop for chisels and one for plane blades, especially as narrower chisels have a tendency to create grooves in the face of the strop.

You can safely test the sharpness of a chisel edge by paring the end grain of wood, especially that of a hard or tough wood. If it cuts cleanly, then the chisel is sharp!

HOW TO USE A LEATHER STROP

After honing a chisel or plane blade, the next stage is to use a strop, a bit like a barber using leather to sharpen a cut-throat razor. The process is simple. Place the blade on the strop at the same angle as its newly honed edge and draw it back towards you using heavy pressure. After six or

seven strokes, turn the blade on its back and again draw it towards you, this time flat against the strop, and again using firm pressure. By pulling the blade towards you rather than pushing away there is no chance of accidentally damaging or tearing the strop. Repeat this process three or four times. If you have honed the edge correctly, stropping will produce a blade as keen as a razor blade, so be careful!

What to Use To Make a Strop

You could use straightforward 3–6mm (⅛–¼in) thick leather with a good face, or, even better, chrome leather, which is pale blue in colour. A little oil will help lubricate it in use. You can buy ready-made strops, which may work better if you use stropping paste, Carborundum powder or some other fine, powdered abrasive to speed up the cutting action. Once you have acquired the habit of using a strop regularly for sharpening tools, you will be amazed at how quickly the quality of your woodwork improves.

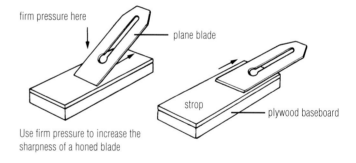

firm pressure here — plane blade — strop — plywood baseboard

Use firm pressure to increase the sharpness of a honed blade

THE SHARPENING STONE

Sharpening stones are either natural or synthetic. The best quality, but unfortunately most expensive, natural stones are Arkansas stones, which are available in three grades. These are known as soft (coarse), hard (medium) and black hard (fine). Synthetic stones are classed as coarse, medium or fine or are available as a combination stone, which contains two different grades of stone, bonded back-to-back. Both natural and synthetic stones rely on oil as the lubricant, whereas a third type, the Japanese water stone, uses water, as its name suggests. A range of diamond stones is also available. These are useful for sharpening tungsten carbide router cutters, as well as chisels and plane blades.

1 Combination oil stone
2 Japanese water stone
3 Diamond sharpening stone
4 Natural sharpening stone

Lubricating Sharpening Stones

For oil stones, use light engineering oil as the lubricant. For water stones, always soak a stone in water before its initial use and never let it freeze as this will cause the stone to crack.

Looking After Your Tools

- Always protect the blade of a bench plane by keeping the plane on its side when not in use. Never use the lever cap to remove the cap iron and plane blade

- Never leave hand tools in a damp atmosphere. Preferably, protect with oiled paper

- Protect chisel and saw blades from damage by using blade covers

- Never use a cutting edge that is not sharp. This is both dangerous and will damage the work, and maybe the tool itself

- Do not use top quality tools on reclaimed timber or over nail heads. Never remove paint with a bench plane or cabinet scraper

- Always re-grind (or have someone else re-grind) plane and chisel blades when honing has removed most of the original grinding edge

TECHNICAL TALK

HONING The final sharpening which produces the cutting edge. Tools can be re-honed as they blunt as long as there is a ground angle left at the end of the plane blade or chisel.

SHOPPING GUIDE

ESSENTIAL TOOL

FINE OR FINE/MEDIUM SYNTHETIC OIL STONE The combination stone gives you two grades, back-to-back

SUGGESTED ADDITIONAL TOOLS

FINE NATURAL SHARPENING STONE A very expensive luxury, but the quality is superb

LEATHER STROP Either buy one or alternatively you can make one yourself (see opposite)

DO'S AND DONT'S

DO	keep the stone flat by moving tools around the face of the stone as you sharpen them
DON'T	let the stone rock or move around while sharpening
DO	keep the stone clean of dirt and grime
DON'T	let the cutting edges of tools dig in and damage the stone
DO	use plenty of pressure while sharpening

TECHNIQUES

Now that you have a kit of basic tools it's time to learn the techniques you need to be able to make a piece of furniture. The pages in this section will take you through the whole process of marking out; planing the wood to make it flat, square, and of uniform thickness; cutting and fitting all kinds of joints, from simple butt joints to more complex dovetails; assembling the pieces of wood and gluing them together; and cleaning up, sanding and finishing.

Work through this section logically: it is worth getting each technique right before you move on to the next. The illustrations are designed to make each technique as clear as possible, and once again there are plenty of tips and technical talk boxes to help you along.

MARKING OUT

TIP

If you have many shoulder lines to mark out (see right) you can hold all the pieces in a vice and mark them out together. Again use the first piece as a template but be careful that the marking lines are all at exactly 90 degrees: even the slightest discrepancy will mean that the shoulder lines will not match each other.

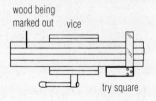

wood being marked out   vice

try square

No matter how much you practise, the fit of a joint can only be as good as the care you take at the marking out stage. If you are measuring where a joint should be, never just guess – instead, make sure that it is put in the right place. The golden rule is – think twice, cut once!

Always work logically following a sequence that makes certain you know where each part goes. Numbering each joint as you progress will prevent mistakes.

Face Side and Face Edge Marks

Once you have selected one face of a piece of wood for its appearance and planed it true and flat, always mark it with a face side mark for ease of identification. Next, when you have made a square edge by working from the face side, mark this with the face edge mark. When you have marked on the face side and face edge, the wood can be gauged to width, planed and then gauged to thickness.

Used properly, face side and edge marks tell you the best face and edge, identify a square corner from which to gauge joints, and allow you to mark out perfect shoulder lines.

Mark on face side first, then face edge.
Next gauge to width. Plane and gauge
to thickness

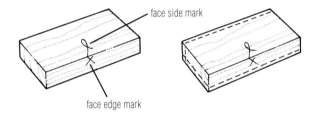

face side mark

face edge mark

HOW TO MARK OUT A SHOULDER LINE

You will need a try square, a marking knife and a pencil. Work from the face side and face edge to produce a perfect line to saw to.

1 Mark on the face side and face edge. If you feel unsure about using a knife to mark shoulders, use a sharp pencil first, and then go over the lines accurately with the knife. Using the try square, work from the face edge and mark a shoulder line on the face side.

2 From the face side, mark a line on the face edge.

3 From the face side, mark a knife line on the edge opposite the face edge.

4 Finally, from the face edge, join up the lines to make a perfect shoulder all around the four surfaces.
Always work the stock of the square from the face side or face edge marks.

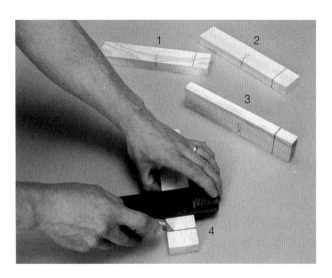

Making Shoulder Lines Match Each Other

Marking on a single shoulder line is simple enough, but what about making up a series of shoulder lines all of which have to match each other, perhaps for a set of bookcase shelves, or maybe rails that will make up the carcase of a piece of furniture?

These are the stages of exactly copying the shoulders on one piece of wood to one or more pieces. Assume in this case that two tenons, 19mm (¾in) long, are to be put on the ends of the rails. Allow for these in the measuring, so that you do not start off with a length of wood that will in the end be too short for the job.

Above: Make up a frame with all the face sides pointing towards you, and the face edges pointing inwards, to guarantee that the joints will match each other. Here the face side marks show the outside of the door – i.e. what you see

65

1 Mark on the first shoulder line from the face edge, allowing more than you need for the tenon.

2 Use a steel rule to establish the exact position of the second shoulder and mark using the end of the knife.

knife point

3 Remove the rule and put the knife point back into the mark it has made.

waste

4 Slide the square up to the knife with the stock of the square on the face edge. Mark on the second shoulder. Use a pencil to establish the length of the tenons. Label the waste.

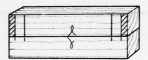

5 Offer up the second piece to the first, marking the position of the shoulders with the end of the knife. Repeat for the other pieces.

6 On each piece use a square to mark on two new shoulder lines. Use a square and knife to continue the shoulders around all four sides (see page 64).

THE BEGINNINGS OF A CABINET

Basic cabinet making may involve making a simple framework, perhaps a door frame intended to fit exactly into an opening. The frame cannot be bigger or smaller than the opening: where do you start?

Measure accurately the internal dimensions of the door opening. Ensure that it is square – if not, allow for any extra and add it to the width

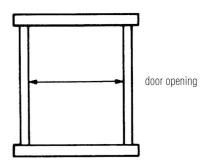

door opening

Measure the width of the stiles and deduct these from the width of the door opening. This will give you the exact length required for the shoulders. Do not forget to allow extra for the joints.

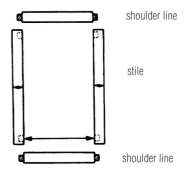

shoulder line

stile

shoulder line

Mark out and cut the shoulder lines accurately. When the joints have been fitted, the door should fit the opening. As a precaution you can allow a little more than the opening on the width – say 1–2mm (1/32in) – to allow for planing to an exact fit later.

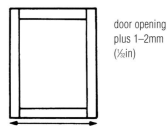

door opening plus 1–2mm (1/32in)

HOW TO USE A MARKING GAUGE

A marking gauge is a simple tool but it takes a little practice to use one properly. Having a point (or two points in the case of a mortise gauge), it is designed to scribe accurate lines along a face or edge. A marking gauge gives a definite groove to work to as it actually scores the wood.

If you are marking across the grain, use a cutting gauge, not a marking gauge. This has a blade which will actually cut the fibres instead of tearing them out. Cutting gauges are used to mark on the shoulders of housing joints.

The two points of a mortise gauge allow you to mark out two parallel lines on the wood simultaneously, at a measured distance from the edge. This gauge is most often used to mark the positions of mortise and tenon joints. The distance between the two pins is easy to adjust; it is usual for this to be the width of the chisel you will use to cut the mortise.

Marking Out

Always work from the face side or face edge to ensure that the joints correspond to each other after cutting.

Hold the gauge in your right hand to give maximum control. Keep the piece of wood being gauged at an angle of 30–45 degrees, either pushing it against a bench stop or holding it securely in a vice. Work the gauge away from you while using light pressure to push against the edge of the wood with the stock. This will help keep it parallel to the edge and stop the point following the grain.

Setting the Distance From the Pin to the Stock

Untighten the thumbscrew on the stock slightly and use a steel rule to measure the exact distance needed between this and the centre of the pin. Hold the stock in your left hand to control it. Tighten the thumbscrew slightly and check the measurement again. If adjusting, gently tap one or other end to move the stock a fraction. When you are satisfied that you have set the gauge correctly, firmly tighten the thumbscrew and double check the measurement.

GOOD ADVICE

Where components are to be marked out as pairs, e.g. on door stiles or the sides of a bookcase (one left-hand, and one right-hand), identify what makes up the pair by writing the information on each piece in pencil. Ensure face side and face edge marks mirror each other, so you cannot make a mistake.

TIP

You can use a pencil to gauge unimportant lines quickly. Hold the pencil firmly and allow your fingers to slide down the edge of the wood.

IMPORTANT

- When using a marking gauge always push it away from you

- Do not use excessive pressure – the face of the wood will tear if you slip

- Do not use too little pressure – you need to create a visible line

- Always work from the face side or face edge marks

- To stop the gauge overshooting, press the point into the wood where you need to finish the line. The tiny pin hole will halt you automatically

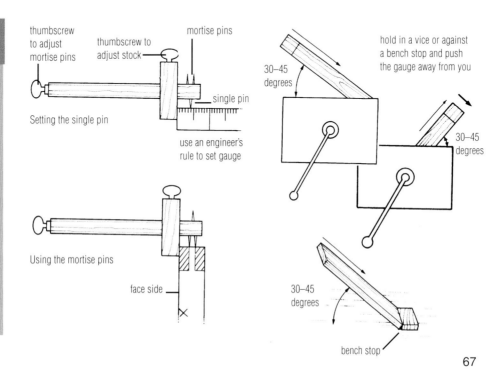

thumbscrew to adjust mortise pins

thumbscrew to adjust stock

mortise pins

single pin

Setting the single pin

use an engineer's rule to set gauge

Using the mortise pins

face side

30–45 degrees

hold in a vice or against a bench stop and push the gauge away from you

30–45 degrees

30–45 degrees

bench stop

THE RIGHT JOINTS FOR THE JOB

You will find specific details on how to mark out, cut and fit important joints on pages 76–88. Whether you are putting up a shelf or working on advanced cabinet making, it is vital to choose the right joint at the outset: decide on the type of joint before cutting the wood to length, ready for marking out.

Most joints, when correctly cut and glued, are strong. If used for the wrong application though (e.g. dowel joints to secure a drawer front) they will soon become weak and fail. Always choose a joint that offers sufficient strength or resistance to pulling or pushing if this is important.

Some joints are easy to mark out and cut, others more difficult. As a rule, the more complex the joint, the stronger it generally is.

Below: Correctly marked out joints with the waste clearly shown ready for removal

1 Bridle joint
2 Stopped, barefaced housing joint
3 Halving joint
4 Mortise and tenon joint
5 Dovetail joint

EASY JOINTS

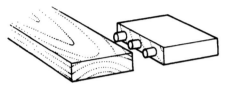

DOWEL JOINT Two pieces of wood held together with long pegs (dowels). The grain runs along the length of the dowel. Offers no resistance to pulling

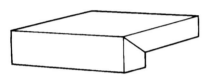

MITRE JOINT A simple joint for corners, usually at 90 degrees. Can be strengthened with glue blocks

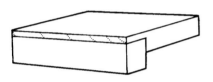

LAP JOINT OR REBATE JOINT A corner joint; one piece covers the other for a more attractive detail than a simple butt joint

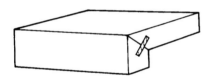

MITRE JOINT WITH LOOSE TONGUE A strengthened mitred joint relying on an inserted piece of wood for extra support

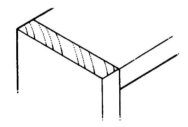

BUTT JOINT Two pieces of wood simply glued together. Two major types: edge-to-edge and corner butt joints. Can be strengthened by using loose tongues or glue blocks

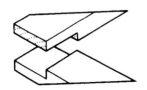

HALVING JOINT Two pieces of wood, with an equal amount of wood cut from each; when interlocked, the overall thickness of the joint equals the amount of wood removed

MORE DIFFICULT JOINTS

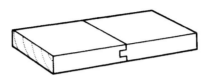

TONGUE AND GROOVE JOINT An edge joint where the tongue on one piece fits into a groove on the other. Sometimes used in panelling or tops, and on unglued flooring to allow for shrinkage

HOUSING JOINT A traditional joint often used in bookcases to fasten a shelf to the side. Main types are through, barefaced and dovetail

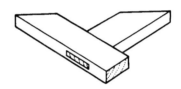

MORTISE AND TENON Most commonly used traditional joint. Very strong, relying on a tight fit for strength. Used for frame and carcase constructions. Through mortise shown

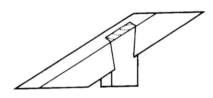

DOVETAILED HALVING JOINT A halving joint with dovetail wedge, producing a very strong shoulder. If pulled, it will tighten itself. A very good frame joint

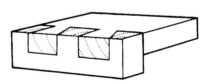

THROUGH DOVETAIL JOINT Wedge-shaped extensions interlock like fingers. Very strong but time consuming to cut and fit

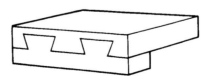

LAPPED DOVETAIL JOINT Dovetail joint where one half extends and covers over the other piece. Used for traditional drawer fronts

PLANING

TECHNICAL TALK

CUP Specific type of warping in wood (see page 14)

INLAY One piece of wood inserted decoratively into another. The inlay is often made up as marquetry

PANEL GAUGE Longer than a standard marking gauge and has a wide stock. Used to gauge wide panels

PARE Trim back to a knife line

SHOOTING BOARD A tool used to steady a piece of wood while cleaning up end grain. Used on conjunction with a try plane and usually fixed at 45 degrees or 90 degrees

WINDING STICKS Two lengths of straight timber, one of which has a black line running along one edge. By placing on a surface and sighting between the two it is easy to spot a board in twist

Although the days of laboriously having to hand plane each and every piece of wood have gone, this does not mean to say that bench planes have been superseded by machines.

Machines are capable of planing vast quantities of wood. This means that they cannot be selective, and planing machines regularly produce defects such as torn grain and cutter marks. This, combined with the fact that most do not guarantee that planed wood will be produced straight and true, means that in terms of quality, bench planes are often able to out-class their larger and more powerful rivals.

Correctly used, bench planes will smooth and flatten wood and will remove most of the defects that machines cause. On the finest quality work, once the wood has been planed by machine, each and every piece should really also be planed by hand.

HOW TO PLANE BOARDS FLAT

Wood is a totally natural material that responds to changes in the moisture content of the atmosphere by either expanding or contracting (see page 9). This means it may well warp or distort in some way as it re-adjusts to new surroundings. If this movement occurs after the wood has been allowed to stabilize by secondary conditioning (see page 10), bench planes are used to flatten the surface of the wood, and prepare it for jointing and sanding.

The Process
Ensure that your workbench top is flat before you start.

1 Place the board to be planed flat on the workbench. It may have already been planed by machine at this stage. Check to see whether it rocks, and if it does (it probably will), put slips of paper or shims underneath the corners to pack out the board and make it artificially flat.

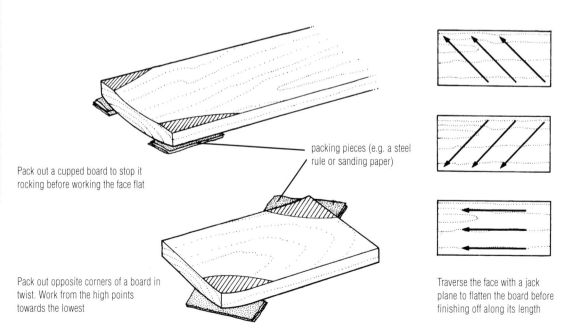

Pack out a cupped board to stop it rocking before working the face flat

packing pieces (e.g. a steel rule or sanding paper)

Pack out opposite corners of a board in twist. Work from the high points towards the lowest

Traverse the face with a jack plane to flatten the board before finishing off along its length

70

2 Next, look at the board to check for any high or low areas, so that you can clearly visualize which parts of the surface need to be worked first.

3 Select either a jack or fore plane that is sharpened and correctly set up for planing boards flat (see page 59).

4 Start by planing the high areas, taking these down to finish, eventually, at the lowest point. Do not put more cut on the plane to try to speed up the process as the plane will simply dig into the wood.

5 Work the whole surface of the board, either along its length or at an angle from its edges (known as traversing – see photograph right). You can work straight across the face if you want to but if you do, take extra care.

6 Try to avoid creating too much torn grain as you work and keep checking to see how much of the surface has been flattened. Finish off along the board's length.

7 When the face is flat, check it, and make this the face side of the board. You can use winding sticks if necessary to check for twist. Next plane an edge, and when you have checked this for square against the face side, mark it up as the face edge.

8 You can now gauge the second edge to width and plane it square to the face side (use a panel gauge on very wide boards).

9 Next, gauge to thickness and plane the other side flat. There should be no need to use packing pieces if you have planed the face side correctly: simply work to the gauge lines.

Note wood that has been prepared with all four surfaces at exactly 90 degrees to each other is known as PSE – Planed Square Edge – or alternatively PAR – Planed All Round. Where the angles are not all at 90 degrees, then the wood is known only as PAR – Planed All Round.

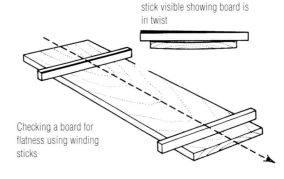

Top edge of back winding stick visible showing board is in twist

Checking a board for flatness using winding sticks

Above: Packers under the corners of a board keep it stable while the whole surface is being traversed planed at around 45 degrees with a jack plane

Check for 'cup' on a board using a pencil and rule. Rub a soft pencil over one edge

of a steel rule and slide it across the face. The pencil marks show the high spots

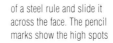

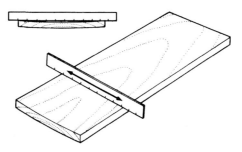

Rub pencil on one edge of rule

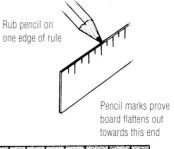

Pencil marks prove board flattens out towards this end

- Plane the edge flat along its length first. Next, concentrate on making it square to the face side.

- One of the biggest problems you will face when you first handle a try plane is mastering the technique of pushing forward, while at the same time carefully moving the plane from one side of the edge to the other. The edges become square as you remove the high areas. Your pencil marks (those put on the edge after checking for square) will show you these high spots, and if your technique is correct they will be completely removed after every one or two strokes. This is why you need to keep checking and re-marking the edge with new pencil marks as you go.

- Ten plane shavings measure, on average, about 1mm (³⁄₆₄in) ... a huge amount of wood! When squaring edges, especially at the final stages, never take off more than two shavings at a time.

SQUARING AN EDGE

After planing the face side of a board flat, the next stage is to produce an edge square to it. Narrower pieces of wood are much easier to work with and with a little practice, you will be able to square an edge very quickly and accurately. You can test how you are going with a try square by putting the stock of the square on the face side and pushing against it. Hold the edge up under a window or in good light to check whether there are any slight gaps – if so, mark them with a pencil.

The illustration on page 73 takes you through the stages of preparing perfectly square edges. You will need a try plane, a try square and a pencil. Note that a correctly sharpened smoothing will not make edges square.

The convex nature of the try plane blade means that by moving the plane from one side of an edge across to the other, the edge will gradually be made square to the face.

WORKING TO A GAUGED LINE

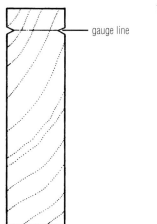

gauge line

feather edge

Plane off the bulk of the wood to within 1–2mm using a fore or try plane. Next take off a shaving or two at a time touching the wood where it needs it

The penultimate shaving will produce a feather edge (tiny sliver of wood) which will fall off. One more shaving will take you to the centre of the gauge line; do not plane beyond this point

Practise Your Planing

A good small project to practise planing edges is to make your own set of winding sticks, which must be perfectly straight (see page 70). These are made from a dry, close-grained hardwood such as beech or maple and should measure around 360mm (15in) long, 33mm (1¼in) wide and 13mm (½in) thick. The back winding stick can be inlaid on its top corner with a dark timber such as American black walnut.

HOW TO PLANE EDGES TO MAKE THEM SQUARE

1 Either plane against a stop or (for edges of wide pieces) put board in a vice. Use a long plane (e.g. a try plane): where the plane touches the edge it will cut; where it does not it will glide over. Don't worry about the edge not being square at this early stage. Always plane from one end to the other

Keep the plane central and keep going until the edge is straight

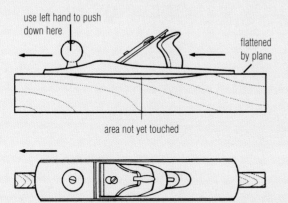

use left hand to push down here

flattened by plane

area not yet touched

2 Next make the edge square: test first with a square and mark high spots on the edge clearly in pencil

face side

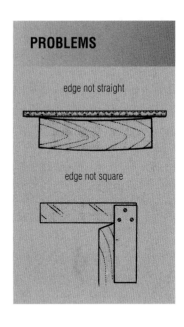

edge not straight

edge not square

3 Move the plane from one side of the edge to the other as you move forward, hitting the high areas. The edge will eventually be made square. Remove 1–2 shavings at a time. Keep checking for square and add new pencil marks as you go

pencil markings (showing the edge is in twist)

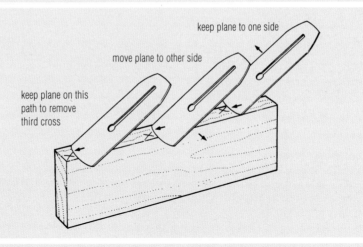

keep plane to one side

move plane to other side

keep plane on this path to remove third cross

4 Used correctly, the convex try plane blade will create a true edge relative to the face side

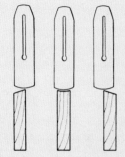

keeping plane to the left removes one side of edge

keeping plane central removes both sides of edge

moving plane to the right removes the other side of edge

5 When the edge is square, finish with one stroke of the plane in a central position

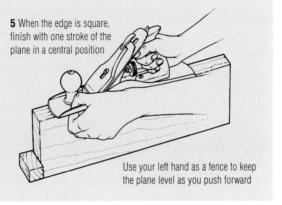

Use your left hand as a fence to keep the plane level as you push forward

Marking position of chamfer:
use left hand to guide and support
plane to produce accurate chamfer

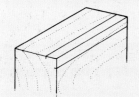

pencil lines show where chamfer
ends; use hand gauging method
(see page 23)

BEVELS AND SPLAYS

Mark both faces rather than work to
an undefined edge

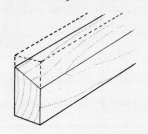

TIP

On wide shelves and panels
plane end grain in one direction,
then turn the wood in the vice
and continue planing in the other
direction.

PLANING END GRAIN

The end grain of wood requires special attention. Imagine wood as being made up of long fibres standing side by side, rather like bristles on a brush. Now visualize the brush being upturned: if you were to stroke the bristles with the palm of your hand, the last bristles, being unsupported, would bend over. Fibres of wood behave just like this. Fortunately there are several ways to stop this being a problem.

Whichever method you choose the main objective when planing end grain is to protect and support the back edge of the wood so it does not spelch out. This also applies to paring with a chisel, boring holes or sawing – always support the waste by using chopping boards, saw boards or blocks.

METHOD 1
use a plane to square off a stile
or rail by working inwards.
Never allow the wood to be
unsupported

METHOD 2
chamfer off a back corner to
give support. Take special
care on the final plane
strokes

METHOD 3
use a scrap piece of wood to
support the back edge

METHOD 4
use a shooting board

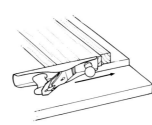

PLANING SIMPLE DECORATIVE MOULDINGS

Rounds, bevels and chamfers are simple mouldings that can be applied to edges to make them look more attractive, or to stop the wood having sharp corners. You can produce them by using special cutters, fitted into a combination plane, or even use an electric router, although the easiest method when preparing only a few decorative edges is the traditional one, using a smoothing plane.

Chamfers

A chamfer runs from one face of a piece of wood to the adjacent edge. Mark the position of the chamfer on the appropriate face and edge in pencil. Do not use a marking gauge, because the lines you create will be difficult to remove. Gauge by hand instead (see page 23).

After marking, you can start to plane. Use your left hand as a guide to steady the smoothing plane, holding it at the same angle as the chamfer. Work the plane backwards and forwards until the bulk of the edge has been removed. Double check that you are working to the correct angle: if you are not, adjust the plane accordingly. Work carefully until you reach the pencil gauge lines.

Splays and Bevels

A splay or bevel is a sloping surface. If it runs from one side of a piece of wood to the other it is best to mark a pencil line on both faces of the wood rather than trying to work to an indefinite top corner. Work in the same way as a chamfer.

Rounds

Rounds can be formed by creating a series of chamfers. Mark on the pencil gauge lines as you would for a single chamfer but also show on both ends of the wood a round of the correct radius. Work this chamfer as normal but do not go all the way down to the pencil gauge lines – just work to the circumference of the round. When you have reached this line you will have created two ridges, so bevel these two corners as though trying to create intermediate splays (see illustrations in box, right), working each one at a time. Do not try to alter the position of the plane in an effort to 'corkscrew' the edge into a round.

Next plane off the new ridges created by the secondary bevels and continue the process, until eventually the ridges left by planing are so small that you can merely sandpaper the edge round. It sounds complicated – but it takes seconds to do!

Sanding Mouldings

If you are having difficulty in sanding a moulding – perhaps you cannot get into a tight corner properly or are damaging other areas of your work – make up a small sanding block which has the reverse profile of the moulding itself. Use a fine or light-weight paper which fits around the block to follow its contours. Use this to sand the moulding along the grain.

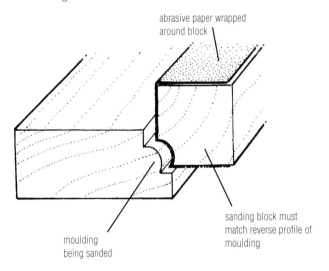

abrasive paper wrapped around block

moulding being sanded

sanding block must match reverse profile of moulding

HOW TO CREATE DECORATIVE MOULDINGS BY HAND

WITH A COMBINATION PLANE

Combination planes produce a variety of mouldings on straight edges, though it can be difficult to stop and start a moulding part-way along an edge. With some methods of frame construction, this can make both the marking out and cutting of the joint quite a complicated process. Also, unlike an electic router, a combination plane cannot easily work mouldings around corners or produce curved work.

SCRATCH STOCK

Usually home-made, a scratch stock consists quite simply of two pieces of wood made into an 'L'-shape, which sandwich a blade in place. The 'L'-shape produces a natural stock to guide the blade and keep it a uniform distance from the edge of the wood being worked.

A scratch stock cuts like a cabinet scraper, with a burr edge acting as a very fine cutter. The problem with using a scratch stock is getting it to cut without roughing up the work. You can make your own mouldings for the blade on a small electric grinding wheel and as long as this burr is pushed along the wood it will cut. If it does not, adjust the angle of the stock until it does.

You can use a scratch stock along the grain for cutting small grooves, for inlays, or for preparing and cleaning up mouldings. When working grooves across the grain, score the wood carefully with a knife first, actually to cut the fibres. The scratch stock then scoops out and removes the wood left between the knife lines.

Cutting mouldings

Cutting grooves

hold scratch stock at a slight angle to help it cut

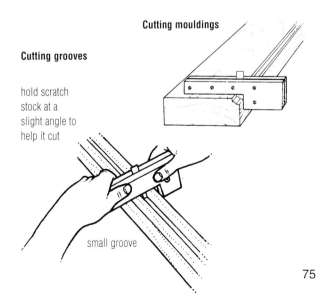

small groove

ROUNDS

position of first chamfer

second intermediate bevel

third bevel produces flat areas so small they can easily be sanded

CUTTING AND FITTING JOINTS

Woodwork joints are mostly held together by interlocking pieces of wood, or adhesives, or both. On some occasions nails or screws may be used, either for speed of assembly or extra strength.

Sometimes, as with dowel or loose tongue joints, a separate piece of wood provides the strength of a joint. In others, such as in a dovetail joint, the strength lies in the way the wood itself is cut.

Joints have evolved into their present day form mainly for two very specific reasons. First, a good fitting joint can be incredibly strong, enhancing the natural properties of wood as a constructional material. Secondly, if it is well proportioned, a joint can also be used as an aesthetic feature in a piece of furniture.

To make properly constructed joints you will need to practise marking out, cutting and fitting different types until you feel confident.

MITRES

Mitres are one of the simplest means of jointing two pieces of wood. This can be at any angle, but this is most often 90 degrees. Mitres are commonly used on picture frames where the joint would be held in place with glue and perhaps strengthened with veneer or panel pins. They are also used on frames, plinths and beads around panels.

It is relatively easy to use a combination square to mark the position of the first halves of two mitre joints on one length of wood, but to copy this information to the other pieces is harder. These guidelines should help.

Marking

After marking the mitres on one piece of wood, put any others to be mitred at the same length one at a time, back to back with the first. Next, mark on the positions of the new mitres with a knife or sharp pencil. Continue these markings around the edges of the wood using the combination square. This will give you an exact line to saw to.

Cutting Out

Put each piece to be cut in a mitre box with the knife line just to one side of the saw slot. Protect the mitre box with a block of scrap wood and hold the wood firmly with your left hand. Always adjust the wood in the box so that the kerf (see page 27) of the saw will run down the waste side of the joint. Make the knife line down the back edge of the mitre bolder if this helps you to produce a clean saw cut.

Let the saw do the work. Do not force it. If you do, the joint will be inaccurate and you could damage the mitre box.

Gluing

When gluing up a mitred frame, use mitre clamps or frame-web clamps. The joints of large, mitred constructions such as plinths on furniture can be strengthened with blocks which are glued, or screwed and glued into place. These are known as glue blocks.

MARKING OUT MITRES

MARKING OUT MITRED RAILS OF EQUAL LENGTH

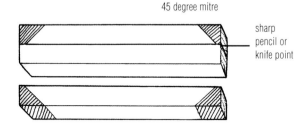

45 degree mitre

sharp pencil or knife point

MARKING OUT MITRES TO FIT A FRAME

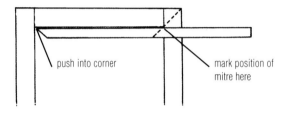

push into corner

mark position of mitre here

TIP

When fitting internal mitred beadings to panels, you can find the exact length you need by sawing one of the mitres first and pushing this into the corner of the frame. This allows you to easily mark the exact position of the second mitre.

USING A MITRE BOX

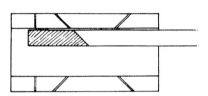

hold the work securely – always saw on the waste side

when using a mitre box you may need to pack out the bottom with scrap wood

GOOD HABITS

- Always mark the waste clearly in pencil. Number the joints

- Use a knife to mark shoulder lines that are to be sawn or pared back to

- Always cut on the waste side of a line, just touching it

- Always hold the work steady and support the waste – use a bench hook or mitre box if appropriate

- Remember that joints can only be as good as the care you take in marking them out

TIP

Cut the longest lengths to be mitred first – then, if you make a mistake, you can cut these down and make them into shorter ones!

TIP

Assemble small frames in a vice if you don't have a mitre or frame clamp. Glue each joint in turn using pins to keep them in place.

DOWEL JOINTS

Dowel joints are simple in concept. A dowel is a cylindrical wooden peg with the grain running along it. This is fastened into two corresponding holes in separate pieces of wood. Once they are held in place with glue, dowels look no different from a traditional mortise and tenon joint, but they are nowhere near as strong. The biggest challenge is making the two holes match each other exactly.

How to Make a Dowel Joint

To join two pieces of wood by use of dowels to make a T-section:

Method One

1 Using a marking gauge, mark a centre line on the end of piece A from the face side.

2 Mark a matching centre line on piece B, again from the face side. Light pencil marks will help you see where to start and stop this centre line.

3 Using a marking gauge, mark measured gauge lines on the end of piece A where the centre of the dowels should be. To ensure that these correspond on piece B, transfer these markings with a knife and square to make a cross, while both pieces are firmly clamped together in a vice.

Method Two

Mark out piece A as in Method One, but drill the holes and then insert centre points into them. Offer up piece B; the centre points will leave tiny pinpoints on piece B in the correct position, ready for drilling.

Method Three

If you need to mark out and cut several dowel joints you can use a dowel jig. One disadvantage is that it may take some time to set up.

Cutting a Dowel Joint

1 Use a metal pointer to make a clear mark at the centre of the crosses on both pieces of wood.

2 Drill both A and B making sure that the holes are exactly at 90 degrees to the marked-out surfaces. A drill stand may help.

3 Fit dowels first to piece A and glue them in place. Ribbed dowels allow glue to escape so that the dowel does not trap the glue as it is pushed home.

4 While the glue is still wet, offer up piece B to piece A and clamp tightly.

Below right: Dowel joints are simple to make and an easy way of fastening two pieces of wood together. Here, pieces A and B are shown marked out ready for drilling (see methods 1 and 2).

1 Dowels
2 Drill bit and drill stop
3 Dowel jig
4 Centre points

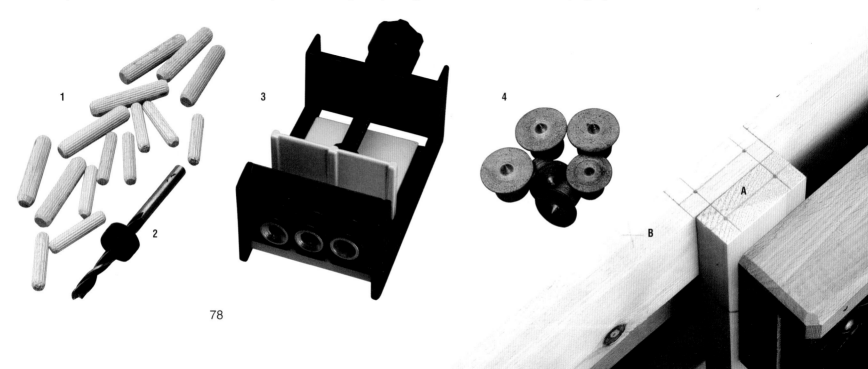

BUTT JOINTS AND EDGE-JOINTING

Butt Joints

A butt joint on a corner couldn't be simpler. It is important to mark the shoulders with a knife (see page 64) and to saw exactly to this line. The saw cut must be accurate, although a light skim with a smoothing plane will produce a cleaner surface for the glue to bond to. Follow the instructions on page 74 to ensure that the grain does not spelch out at the back.

Where extra strength is needed it is wise to use glue blocks. These can be glued in place or screwed and glued: either way, they strengthen the joint. In furniture making, this sort of butt joint is most often used for the back joints of a plinth assembly.

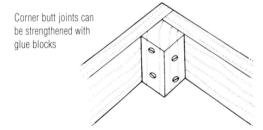

Corner butt joints can be strengthened with glue blocks

Dovetail Nailing

Butt joints can be strengthened by dovetail nailing, where nails are driven into the joint at alternating angles. Insert the first nail at the centre of the joint, square-on, to stop the butt joint moving around. Then dovetail nail on either side of the first nail.

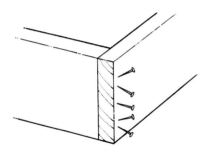

Edge-Jointing

The illustration on page 73 shows how to plane one edge perfectly square. Edge jointing two boards together relies on preparing two edges in this way, and then fitting them together.

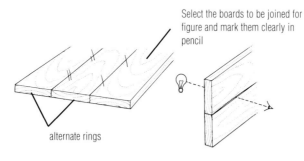

Select the boards to be joined for figure and mark them clearly in pencil

alternate rings

Check that they join exactly using natural or artificial light behind the joint. If there is a tiny gap take off one more shaving

Use a straight edge to check the joined boards lie straight and do not lean

A good edge joint (sometimes known as a rub joint) should not rely on tongues or dowels to keep it together. When complete, the joint should hardly be visible and you certainly should not see any trace of a glue line.

Select the pieces of wood to be jointed for their attractive figure, and if you can, fit the boards together with the growth rings arranged alternately for stability: by doing this, if there is a slight amount of movement, both boards will cup in different directions, making the boards much easier to flatten again with hand planes. Mark the boards with a pencil line to show where they go and prepare the edges with a try plane. Next, put one of the pieces in the vice and offer the other one up to it. Have some light behind the joint to help you see whether there are any gaps between the two boards. Adjust the piece held in the vice as necessary by taking off just one or two shavings with the try plane. This is not difficult but perfecting the technique takes some practice. While they are still in the vice, make sure that the two boards sit perfectly on top of each other and do not lean. You can check this with a straight edge.

Edge-Jointing – a Second Method

This method is suitable for short lengths of wood only, and it relies on the convex nature of the plane blade. Put both pieces of wood together in a vice and plane them both at the same time. Remove them from the vice and turn one of them over: they should fit together, to produce a very quick butt joint.

TIP

At first you may not feel confident enough to rely solely on an edge butt joint and you may prefer to strengthen it. Here are some ways you could try

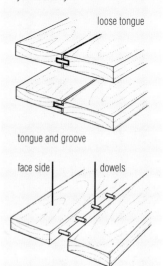

loose tongue

tongue and groove

face side   dowels

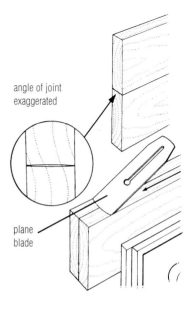

angle of joint exaggerated

plane blade

79

THE MORTISE AND TENON JOINT

The mortise and tenon joint is perhaps 'the' most basic woodwork joint. It utilizes the strength of wood by interlocking one piece of wood with another.

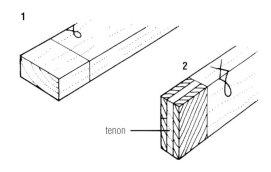

Marking Out a Single Mortise and Tenon Joint

Below: Mortise and tenon joints can take many forms. Here are a few:

1 Loose wedge mortise and tenon
2 Moulded groove frame mortise and tenon
3 Stopped mortise and tenon
4 Through mortise and tenon

1 Mark four shoulder lines with a knife on the piece that is to have the tenon. Work from the face side and face edge (see page 64).

2 Use a mortise gauge, set up to the width of your mortise chisel to mark the position of the tenon. This should be roughly central and about a third of the total thickness of the wood. Show the waste clearly.

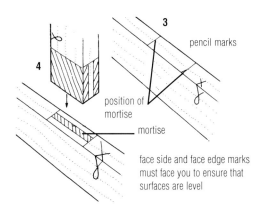

3 Mark the length of the mortise on the second piece with light pencil lines. You can use the width of the tenon as a template, which will help you to establish the length of the mortise.

4 Go over the pencil lines with a knife to show clearly the position of the mortise. Use the mortise gauge at the same setting as the tenon to mark on the width of the mortise. Work from the face sides on both pieces, so that the tenon corresponds to the mortise. Again mark the waste.

Cutting Out

Once the joint has been marked out you can start cutting. The quality of the finished joint depends very much on how good you are at using a saw and chisel. Follow the gauge lines, correcting yourself as soon as possible if you wander from the line. Do not rush, work carefully and do not allow the saw to bind. A little paraffin wax will help the saw blade to cut smoothly. Keep checking as you saw that you do not go past the marking gauge lines.

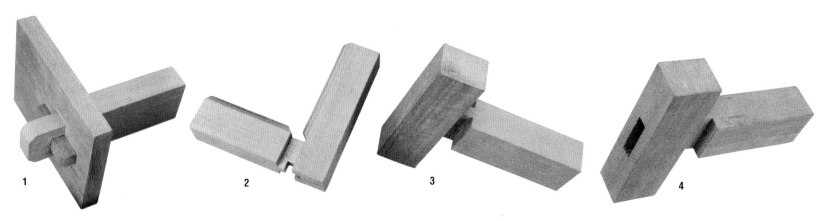

HOW TO CUT THE TENON

1 Put the piece of wood with the tenon marked on it into a vice at an angle of around 45 degrees. Standing sideways to the bench front, use a tenon saw to cut down to the shoulder line facing you. Cut down both cheeks of the tenon while in this position.

2 Turn the piece of wood around and (again at around 45 degrees in the vice) cut both cheeks of the tenon from the other edge.

3 Now saw fully down to the shoulder line. This time, hold the wood upright in the vice and continue sawing down the saw cuts you have already made, being careful not to go past the shoulder line, especially at the back.

4 Next, use a bench hook to support the work and cut the shoulders. Remove the waste pieces which will fall off as you saw. A 'V' will help you start sawing (see page 26).

5 Clean up the corners of shoulders carefully with a chisel to ensure a flush fit.

1

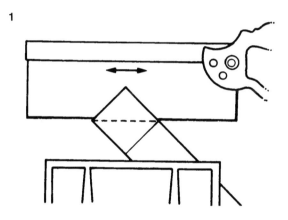

2

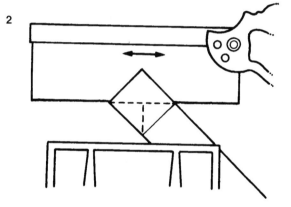

3

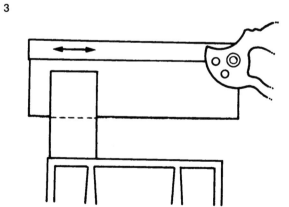

4

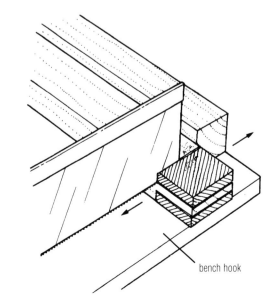

bench hook

HOW TO CUT A MORTISE BY HAND

1 Hold the work on the bench securely with an F or G-clamp, protecting it with an offcut of wood. Protect the bench too, with another offcut used as a cutting board.

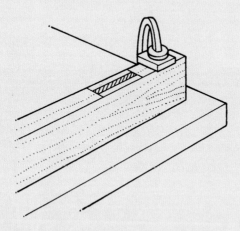

2 (A–D) Use a mortise chisel and mallet to cut the mortise, as shown below.

A start in centre with chisel upright

B work towards you cleaning out the waste

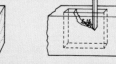

C turn chisel around and work away from you again cleaning out the waste

D with the mortise hole clear of waste make a final clean cut down each shoulder line

Be careful as the chisel may creep back slightly as you cut.

3 Make sure that the bottom of the mortise is clean and flat, checking with a depth gauge if necessary. The mortise should be around 2mm (1/16in) deeper than the length of the tenon. This will avoid a 'glue trap' which may prevent the joint being pushed together during assembly.

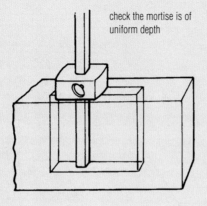

check the mortise is of uniform depth

Fitting

There is usually a little cleaning up to do after sawing, the biggest problems being the shoulders of the tenon and the bottom of the mortise. If both halves of the joint are accurately cut, they should fit snugly together. If they do not, check to find out why and adjust them accordingly.

CLEANING UP FOR FITTING

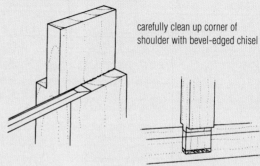

carefully clean up corner of shoulder with bevel-edged chisel

clean out waste or joint will not fit

HALVING JOINT

A halving joint is so-called because in theory you remove half the thickness of each piece of wood, so that each part fits snugly into the other. There are three variations – the cross halving, the T-halving and the corner halving

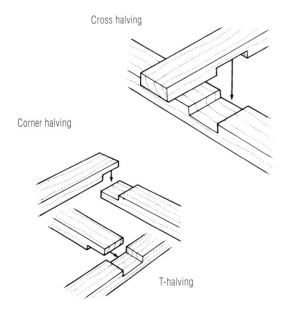

Cross halving

Corner halving

T-halving

cut

turn wood around

clean up bottom of joint

How to Mark Out a Cross Halving Joint

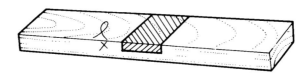

always mark from face side

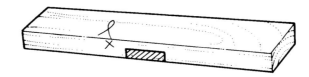

Working from the face side and edge, mark out the shoulder lines of the halving joint on each of the two pieces of wood. Put the knife-lines on one face and two edges. Note that one piece will have knifed markings on its face side while the other will have knife lines on the side opposite the face side.

To establish the width of the joint, use one half as the template to guarantee that both will fit each other exactly.

Next, use a marking gauge set to about half the thickness of the wood. It does not need to be exact, as long as both pieces match each other later. This is guaranteed by working from the face sides. You must use only one setting on the gauge to ensure both halves fit.

How to Cut a Halving Joint

Saw each shoulder line in turn holding it against a bench hook. Work on the waste side, cutting down to gauged shoulder lines, but do not go past them.

Now hold the timber in a vice, and using a bevel-edged chisel (bevel down), remove part of the waste. After working from one side, turn the wood around and work from the other side.

Finish off by cleaning up to the marking gauge line, by horizontal paring with the chisel, this time, bevel up (see page 44).

BRIDLE JOINT

The bridle joint has two common forms, the corner bridle joint and the 'T' bridle joint. They are marked out in a similar way to mortise and tenon joints.

The corner bridle joint has a straightforward tenon on one half, which is cut using the same technique as that shown on page 81. The other half of the joint (known as the mortise) is best cut out as follows.

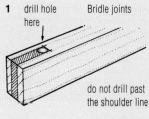

1 drill hole here   Bridle joints

do not drill past the shoulder line

After marking on the position of the mortise, drill a hole near the shoulder line the same width as, or a little less than, the mortise itself.

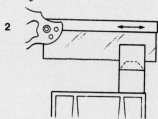

2

Saw the cheeks as you would saw a tenon, eventually meeting up with the hole.

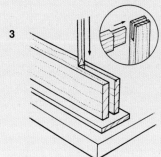

3

Clean up the bottom of the mortise with a bevel-edged chisel, working from both edges so that you don't tear out the wood on the back edge.

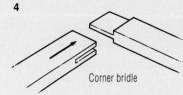

4

Corner bridle

Check that the joint fits and adjust accordingly.

How to Cut a 'T' Bridle Joint

Cut the mortise as for a corner bridle joint. Cut the tenon as for a halving joint – but instead of working to half the thickness with a marking gauge, you will have to work to a third of the thickness and use a mortise gauge.

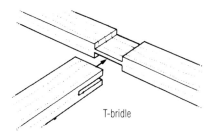

T-bridle

HOUSING JOINT

Housing joints are often used on traditional bookcase shelving. There are two variations on the normal through housing – the barefaced housing and the dovetailed housing. Housing joints are either cut as through joints, or 'stopped' so that the joint is not seen on the front edge of a carcase.

How to Mark Out a Through Housing Joint

On a through housing the shelf-part of the joint is marked out like a simple butt joint. Measure the length of the shelf and use a knife and square to mark two sets of knife lines around all four surfaces. Mark on the waste. Ensure that after cutting, all ends are square and of the same length.

On the component to become the bookcase side, mark the top position of the joint using a sharp pencil and try square, lining in with a knife. Continue these lines in pencil only, to roughly half-way down the front and back edges. Then use the shelf as a template to establish the exact width of the joint, marking this position too. From the face side, mark the depth (about one third to one half the thickness) of the housing joint on the back and front edges with a marking gauge, using the pencil lines as a guide to how far to go. Go over the pencil lines with a knife and mark on the waste.

Barefaced Housing Joint

On a barefaced housing, after cutting the shelf to length, lightly plane the ends and use a cutting gauge to mark on the shoulders of the joint. The thickness of the joint is marked on the end using a marking gauge.

How to Cut a Housing Joint

Use a tenon saw to cut the sides of the trench and remove the centre of the joint by using a hand-held router plane (see tip, right). If the joint is stopped, cut a mortise at one end of the trench first to saw into. When using the saw to cut the trench, clamp on a piece of wood just to one side of the knife-line to act as a guide. Always saw on the waste side. If you prefer you could use an electric router held against a stop that is clamped in place, but work carefully and slowly so that you do not slip.

TYPES OF HOUSING JOINT

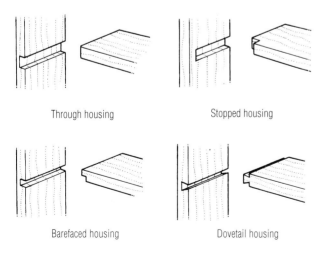

Through housing   Stopped housing

Barefaced housing   Dovetail housing

MORE COMPLEX JOINTS

The Dovetail Joint

The dovetail joint is one of the strongest and most decorative joints of all. There are many sorts of dovetail joint, but the two most common types are those used on drawers, namely the through dovetail (at the back) and the lapped dovetail (at the front).

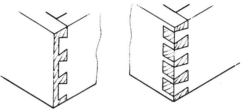

Lapped dovetail (as used at front of drawers)   Through dovetail (as used at back of drawers)

Marking Out the Through Dovetail Joint

The through dovetail is quite easy to mark out as long as you follow a logical procedure.

Let us use a drawer as an example. The width of this drawer is 100mm (4in) and there are to be three dovetails. (Usually the number of dovetails is a matter of personal choice.) The width of the pins is to be 6mm (¼in) – which is the width of the chisel you will use to remove them later. The width of the side pins is to be 8mm (⅝in).

MARKING THE DOVETAILS

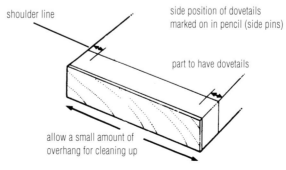

shoulder line

side position of dovetails marked on in pencil (side pins)

part to have dovetails

allow a small amount of overhang for cleaning up

Above: A stopped barefaced housing joint is a neat, strong joint for shelving

TIP

If you prefer, when cutting a trench on a housing joint, you could use an electric router held against a stop that is clamped in place. Work carefully and slowly so you do not slip.

MARKING OUT A THROUGH DOVETAIL JOINT

Below: Knife lines on joints should be crisp, accurate and deep enough to cut the fibres of the wood

You will need a 6mm (¼in) bevel-edged chisel, two pairs of dividers, a pencil and a knife. Always keep the face sides of all pieces making up the drawer pointing inwards. Mark shoulder lines on both pieces to be jointed, allowing around 0.5mm (½2in) overhang for cleaning up. On the piece that is to have the dovetails, mark out as follows:

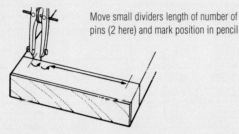

Move small dividers length of number of pins (2 here) and mark position in pencil

1 Set up one of the pairs of dividers to the width of the 6mm (¼in) bevel-edged chisel that will be used to cut out the pins, plus 0.5mm (½2in) (to allow for clearance). From the left-hand 8mm (⅝6in) pencil line marking the position of the end pin, use the dividers to count two 6mm (¼in) 'spaces'. Mark this position with the point of a sharp pencil.

Fact: the space that is now left between this pencil point and the right-hand side pin is exactly the same as the combined length of the three dovetails you need. If you divide this space into three, it will equal the width of one of the dovetails.

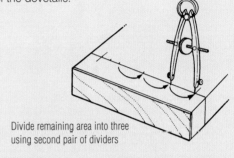

Divide remaining area into three using second pair of dividers

2 Take the second pair of dividers and set them to what you estimate a third of this space to be, then adjust the dividers slightly until they are actually set at the correct width: this should only take seconds!

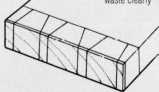

Use one pair of dividers to mark on the pin, the other pair the dovetail – keep alternating along the shoulder line

3 Next mark on the position of the first dovetail, starting from the left-hand side pin, using the second pair of dividers. Then mark on a pin (with the first pair of dividers), then a dovetail, then a pin, and finally a third dovetail. You will finish exactly at the position of the right-hand side pin. Mark the points clearly with the end of a knife as you go and you will easily see where the two pins and three dovetails should be.

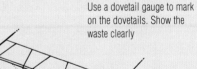

Use a dovetail gauge to mark on the dovetails. Show the waste clearly

4 After this, hold the wood upright in a vice and use a dovetail gauge and knife to mark out the dovetails, both on the face of the wood and across the end too. Mark the waste clearly.

How to Cut a Through Dovetail

So far, you have marked out the dovetails for only one half of a dovetail joint. Cut these out before marking out the pins for the second piece of wood.

Hold the wood in a vice and saw each dovetail on the waste side down to the shoulder. Keep checking at the back that you have not gone too far.

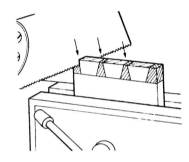

Saw one set of angles and then alter your position to cut the second set

Remove the 8mm (⅜in) end pins from each side with a tenon saw. On the bench chop out the two central pins with the 6mm (¼in) chisel, paring back cleanly to the line from one face only. Use a chopping board to stop the wood spelching out at the back.

Once you have cut out the dovetails for this half of the joint you can use it as an exact template for the other half. It is crucial that you remember to number all joints clearly.

How to Mark Out the Pins

Lay a flat packing piece – say a square piece of 12mm (½in) thick plywood – on the bench. Hold the piece to be marked out in a vice with the face side facing away from you. Let it protrude from the vice so that it is the same height as the packing piece. Place the other half of the joint, with the dovetails already cut, face side down on top of the piece in the vice, so that it rests both on this piece and on the packing piece. Now use a knife to mark the corresponding pins on the piece of wood in the vice. Push your left hand down on the wood to stop it moving about as you mark out the joint. Leave a tiny gap at the shoulder of the joint between the two pieces, so that you can just see light through it as you look down. This will allow for 'creep' later, when cutting out the joint. When you take the top piece off you will see the exact outline of the joint. Follow these knifed lines down to

the shoulder line with a sharp pencil to help you saw accurately. Remember to mark on the waste.

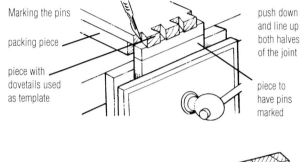

Marking the pins

packing piece

piece with dovetails used as template

push down and line up both halves of the joint

piece to have pins marked

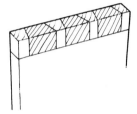

After making out the pins, cut out with a dovetail or tenon saw

QUICK METHOD FOR MARKING OUT THROUGH DOVETAILS

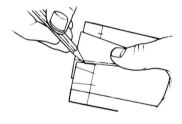

When marking out dovetail joints it is essential that the pins and tails are properly spaced and that their sizes are uniform. The above method guarantees this and is especially suitable for deep drawers, boxes and chests. There is an alternative, quick, method:

After marking on the positions of the side pins as normal, simply divide the space left into the number of dovetails required (use a rule at a slight angle across the face to measure off the correct spaces if necessary) and mark these positions on the shoulder line using a sharp pencil. Next, on either side of these pencil lines, measure half the distance of the bevel-edged chisel you are using, and mark the pins. Do not forget to add a little to the measurement to stop the chisel binding as you cut the pin. Use a dovetail gauge to continue these lines around the end and face as for the method above.

87

TECHNICAL TALK

CREEP The small distance a chisel wanders from a knife line due to its bevelled cutting edge

CUTTING BOARD (chopping board) Scrap piece of wood used to protect the bench top while chopping out joints. It must be smooth, flat and undamaged to protect the workpiece

DOVETAIL BLOCK Clamping block with finger-like extensions which push dovetails into place, allowing pins to fit in-between

DOVETAIL GAUGE Tool used to guarantee a uniform angle

DOVETAILS AND PINS Two halves of a dovetail joint. Dovetails are wedge-shaped extensions, usually wider than the pins, which are the slender extensions that fit into the gap (eye or socket) between the dovetails

FLUTED DOWEL Dowel that is ribbed along its length, allowing glue to escape

PARAFFIN WAX White-coloured wax used for candle-making. Ideal for lubricating wooden components (e.g. drawers); and waxing saw blades and plane soles

TRENCH A long, narrow groove running across the grain of a piece of wood

How to Cut Out the Pins

Saw down the pencil lines on the waste side to the shoulder, holding the workpiece in a vice. Remove the waste carefully with a coping saw, leaving around 2mm (1/16in) to the shoulder. Clean this up by vertical paring back to the shoulder with a bevel-edged chisel.

The Lapped Dovetail

Cut the wood to be joined to length and then mark out the tails as you would a through dovetail joint (it is not necessary to allow any overhang), but ensure that the ends are perfectly square, as they are to be used as a template.

When marking out the pins, work in the vice as before, again using a packing piece, but this time, use your knife to mark all the way around the dovetails – i.e. along the length of the dovetails as well as across their width.

After marking on the waste, saw down the marking lines on the waste side at an angle of around 45 degrees, using a bevel-edged chisel to chop out the rest of the joint.

GOOD ADVICE

- Always fit joints (or tap them apart) with a hammer, not a mallet, and use a protective block. Do not try to pull joints apart by hand, especially dovetails and mortise and tenons as they easily damage.

- Always work exactly to the knifed shoulder lines and expect the chisel to creep slightly when cutting out. Double check that you have removed all the waste from the bottoms of joints (especially in tight corners) as it is never a wise policy to rely on trying to force a joint into place.

- When putting dovetails together, test whether they will work by pushing them only part-way in – never more than half-way.

- Always support the work properly and always cut on the waste side.

- When gluing up very tight dovetail joints you can use dovetail blocks to help push the joints into place (see page 93).

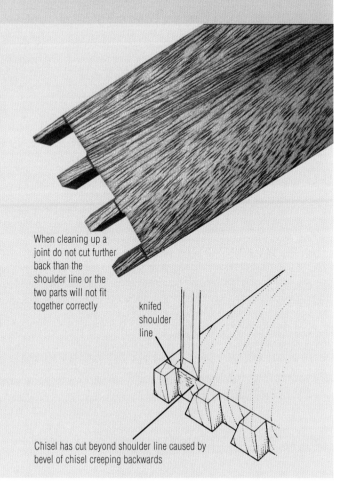

When cleaning up a joint do not cut further back than the shoulder line or the two parts will not fit together correctly

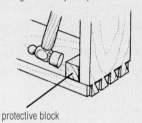

Taking a dovetail joint apart

protective block

knifed shoulder line

Chisel has cut beyond shoulder line caused by bevel of chisel creeping backwards

ASSEMBLING AND GLUING UP

It is at the gluing up stage that theory is put into instant practice. Rushing around and wiping glue off with damp cloths is all part of the job – but there's no need to panic.

When you are ready to assemble a piece of furniture it is a good idea to do a trial glue-up (dry assembly) first. This will allow you to ensure that everything goes together as it should and that you have the right tools, such as clamps, to hand.

How to Carry Out a Dry Assembly

As the purpose of the trial run is to make sure things fit, before you start you should check that all joints are properly cleaned out and that they have been cut exactly to the marking out lines. Then put everything together, following the numbers on your joints. Next identify any offending joint or area that needs more attention, take everything apart again and adjust it. If you are still not sure that the joints will go together, do a second dry assembly.

The more experienced you become, the more this trial glue-up will be of use in making sure that you have everything to hand for gluing rather than for checking the joints. But for a beginner, this stage can make all the difference in the world to the look of the finished piece.

When gluing up it is always a good idea to have someone with you to hold and steady long sash clamps and clamping blocks, as they can easily be the cause of dents and bruises on wood.

Clamping Blocks

Your clamping blocks should all be of the same thickness, so check that they fit in the clamps. Make sure they are all clean and undamaged. They should not be made of a harder material than the wood you are about to to glue up – for example, do not use oak blocks to glue up softwood furniture.

As well as clamps and clamping blocks, you also need a few pointed scrapers (homemade wooden ones are handy), some rags and a bucket of water, for wiping off the glue.

Below: Gluing up a simple frame – sash clamps and clamping blocks are shown in position. Always have a bucket of water and a cloth handy for wiping down

1 Squaring rod
2 Steel rule
3 Tape measure
4 Steel and wooden pointers for removing excess glue
5 Try square

Right: After gluing a simple frame together, check that it is square and flat (see below) and adjust if necessary. Leave to dry

GLUING A SIMPLE FRAME

Assembling and gluing up a simple frame construction, such as a door with traditional mortise and tenon joints, is quite straightforward. Bookcases and other pieces of furniture with more complicated constructions can be more troublesome.

For a simple frame, first prepare the sash clamps and blocks and lay them out at roughly the right distance apart from each other on a floor or flat surface. Put the (as yet unglued) frame components in their relevant positions so that there is no confusion over where each one goes.

One of the easiest adhesives to use is PVA (see page 93), which is white in colour. When dry, it produces a very strong bond on bare wood, as long as it is clean and free from oil and grease.

Apply PVA adhesive to one half of the joint only, or in accordance with manufacturer's instructions. With mortise and tenon joints it is best to squeeze it into the mortise. Do not be too liberal: if you use too much glue at this stage you will despair later, when glue is running everywhere or when you cannot put a joint together because of trapped glue.

Make sure that all surfaces of the joint are well covered with adhesive by using a pointed stick to spread it around evenly. You have about 15 to 20 minutes to apply the glue and assemble the frame, so there is no need to rush.

After applying the adhesive, assemble the frame and put it in the clamps, which are ready and waiting. Move the clamps a little if necessary so that they are in exactly the right position, and insert the clamping blocks. Gently tighten each clamp until it starts to bite. You will find that some glue oozes out at this stage: before clamping up too tightly, wipe this off. Don't forget to check underneath! Now clamp up more tightly, checking for square (see below) and adjusting if necessary. Next, wipe off the rest of the glue. Leave the frame to dry for at least 24 hours, or longer if possible.

CHECKING FOR SQUARE

During gluing, but before the frame has dried, you must guarantee that it is square and flat. To check this you can use some of these simple techniques.

1 Ensure your try square is accurate. Use internal corners to check the frame for square

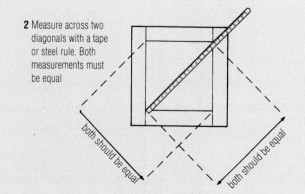

frame

small gap

small gap

try square

2 Measure across two diagonals with a tape or steel rule. Both measurements must be equal

both should be equal

both should be equal

3 If it is difficult to check an internal measurement, use one or two pointed pieces of wood – squaring rods – pushed tight into the corners. The frame is square when opposite diagonals measure the same

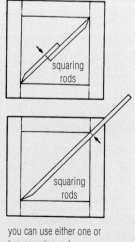

squaring rods

squaring rods

you can use either one or two squaring rods

GLUING UP MORE COMPLEX PROJECTS

Being organized when gluing up difficult constructions makes all the difference.

Assembling a simple frame is relatively easy because there are only four right-angles to check. Also, you have plenty of time before the adhesive becomes unworkable. This may not be so with more complex projects.

You will need to handle all the clamps and other tools you use during gluing quickly, but carefully. Take extra care not to damage anything as you work.

As an example, assume that you are gluing up the bookcase shown in the projects section of this book, on page 118. In this particular case, the best procedure for gluing is as follows.

Prepare your clamps (see page 89). Lay one bookcase side on the floor and apply glue to the housing joints and mortises. Use a small stick to spread the glue around the joints. Repeat for the other bookcase side.

Next, insert the shelves and rails into one of the sides – let gravity do the work for you! Now comes the tricky part: preferably with the help of someone else, quickly lift and turn the second bookcase side over and locate the relevant joints, tapping them into place with the palm of your hand. On some projects you may have several joints to locate, so you must work quickly to stop the glue running out of the joints.

When you have located all the joints, turn the bookcase on its back and sit it on the prepared sash clamps. Gently tighten them with clamping blocks in place. Put more clamps on the front of the bookcase and gently tighten them. Wipe off any excess glue, and then fully tighten all clamps. Check for square.

With bookcases or wide components you may find that the centre of the sides actually bellies outwards as the clamps are tightened. This is caused by trapped glue or air and can be cured by the use of cauls – curved clamping blocks which are designed to increase the pressure at the centre of the bookcase side (see illustrations, page 93). You can cut these cauls yourself.

Chairs and other awkward shapes are usually best supported with frame clamps or web clamps, or even a loop of string tightened with a stick. Drafting tape will help keep small components in place as they dry.

Finally, do not be afraid to hit a joint (protected by a block) quite firmly with a hammer to knock it into place. However, before you use the hammer, make sure that the only reason for the joint not going home is because it is a good tight fit. If not, you are likely to hear a stomach-churning splitting sound …

Gluing up more complex projects can occasionally become quite a hectic experience, but if you are prepared for all eventualities by careful organization and especially by performing a dry assembly first, then things should run smoothly and work according to plan.

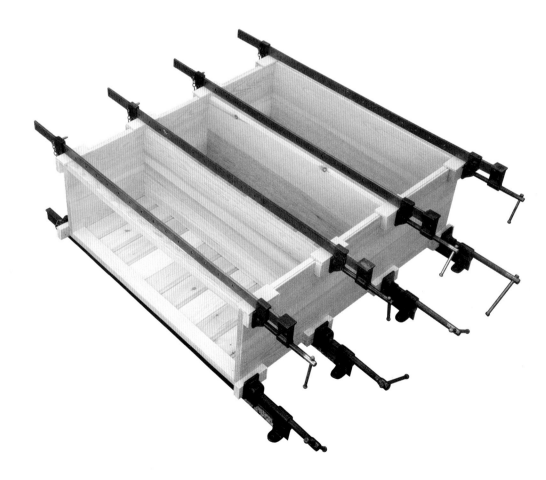

Below: Sash clamps holding a complex carcase together during a dry assembly. Make sure that all clamps are directly in line with the shelves, base and top rails as shown

HOW TO GLUE EDGE JOINTED BOARDS

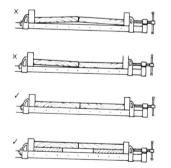

sash clamps on top help keep boards flat

first set of sash clamps hold the boards from below

1 If you use wood that has been planed on two faces, it is easy to select boards for matching figure. Prepare the edges to be jointed for gluing (see page 79). Mark these faces clearly with a pencil.

2 Put sash clamps on the floor, with their centres 450–600mm (18–24in) apart. Long boards may need several clamps.

3 Lay the boards on the clamps and dry clamp them to ensure the joints are good and will go together.

4 Undo the clamps and apply PVA adhesive to one edge only of each joint. Leave the adhesive for about 3–4 minutes to change colour from white to pale grey, but do not let it dry out.

5 Clamp the boards together again and wipe off any excess glue. There may be a slight amount of 'bellying

up' as you clamp up. This can be rectified by adding more clamps in-between the others, but on top of the boards, rather than below. Make sure the boards lie flat on the bottom clamps. Some woods, such as oak, may discolour because of a chemical reaction between the wood and the glue. If this is a problem, use spacers between the clamps and the wood, making sure they are of equal thickness to ensure the wood remains flat.

If the boards are still not flat, or if the problem is extreme, the probable fault is that the edges have not been planed square. If this is the case, the only remedy is to go back to the workbench and practise your planing.

After gluing, leave the boards to dry, then remove the panel from the clamps. Clean up the faces with a smoothing plane (see page 95). If there has been a slight amount of distortion during gluing up, you can rectify this by lightly working over the surface first with a jack or fore plane.

Gluing panels and tops – keep boards flat on clamps or spacers of equal thickness

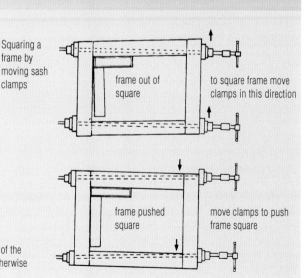

HOW TO CORRECT OUT-OF-SQUARE FRAMES

When you first use sash clamps they should lie straight along the line of the joint. Sometimes, though, you will need to put a clamp at an unusual angle to push a frame into square. We may only be talking of 2mm (⅟₁₆in) or less, but it is best to sort out any problems while the glue is still wet.

The rules of adjusting and checking for square are the same for both simple frames and larger carcase constructions such as the bookcase. You may only need to move one or two of the clamps rather than all of them, but if there are several clamps on the piece you are adjusting, it is a good idea to loosen them all very slightly to help the adjustment take place. After making the adjustments, always check the carcase for square again.

Where to put champing blocks on frames

Sash clamps should always lie along the line of the joint unless squaring the frame determines otherwise

Squaring a frame by moving sash clamps

frame out of square

to square frame move clamps in this direction

frame pushed square

move clamps to push frame square

92

HOW TO GLUE DOVETAIL JOINTS

Dovetail joints may be glued together using clamps like other joints, or they can be left unclamped if the joint is fully together and tight. If you do clamp them, it is a good idea to make up a set of dovetail clamping blocks, which will deliver increased force where it is needed. Apply PVA adhesive to the half of the joint with the pins, spreading it on all internal faces. Assemble the work and use sash clamps and clamping blocks to clamp up from the centre dovetail. Clamp alternate dovetails one at a time, working towards the edges. Once the joint is pushed home (a hammer and block may help stubborn joints), clamp up again tightly along the line of the centre of the joint.

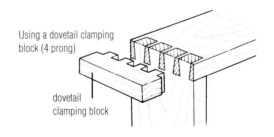

Using a dovetail clamping block (4 prong)

dovetail clamping block

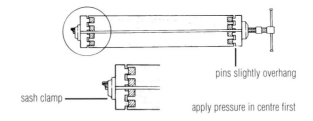

pins slightly overhang

sash clamp

apply pressure in centre first

TYPES OF ADHESIVE

As the chemistry of adhesives is complex, the descriptions here offer a basic guide and so are not clouded in technical jargon. For general woodwork there are four basic types: scotch/pearl glue, suitable for internal woodwork only; PVA (emulsion) adhesive; two-part adhesive, and impact/contact adhesive. There are also 'hot-melt' glues used in glue guns – these are suitable for veneer work.

PVA (emulsion) Adhesive
PVA is available in formulations suitable for either external or internal work. It is strong and very easy to use. Allow 15–20 minutes of working time during assembly. Beware, though – if the glue is allowed to dry on bare wood, white marks become highly visible on subsequent polishing.

Scotch/Pearl Glue
A traditional glue made from animal hide and bone. Also known as animal glue. Suitable for use on internal parts only, and usually bought in the form of pearls. Soak these pearls first in water, before heating in a glue pot. Scotch glue is easy to sand off the surface of wood and generally does not mark the work. Any glue left in the pot can simply be reheated, making it immediately ready for use again. The disadvantage of animal glue is that it is not particularly strong (certainly not as strong as PVA) and as it cools and

gels very quickly it can make the gluing up of larger projects difficult.

A major bonus for furniture restorers working on older pieces that have been glued with Scotch glue, is that the gentle heat from a hair dryer or a little warm water in a syringe will easily soften the glue again. Thus the joints can be taken apart for repair and reglued. Decorative inlays and bandings are usually glued in place with animal glue.

Two-Part Adhesive
This term covers dozens of adhesives, including urea formaldehyde, resorcinol and epoxy resins. The adhesive comes in two parts, a resin and a hardener, and the mixing of these in specific ratios produces a reaction, giving each adhesive its own properties. Two-part adhesives are often used where extremely strong glue bonds are required, some being especially suited to very heavy duty work.

Impact/Contact Adhesive
The most suitable type of adhesive for bonding plastic laminate or for small areas of veneer work. Thinly spread the glue on both faces and leave a short while for it to become tacky. The glue bond is either formed the second the two faces meet or as soon as pressure is applied, depending on the particular adhesive. Whatever happens, do not put veneer in the wrong place if working with impact adhesive, or you will regret it!

TIP

HOLDING AWKWARD SHAPES
It is easy to rig up your own holding devices for awkward shapes

as string is tightened components are pulled together

Putting extra pressure where needed on wide components (e.g. bookcase sides)

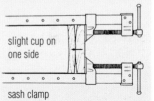

slight cup on one side

sash clamp

use a curved clamping block (caul) to push the centre of the side into position

Note above illustration is shown in section.

CLEANING UP

No matter how carefully you have made your joints, after gluing there are bound to be some parts of a construction that are not quite flat or level. Cleaning up puts these slight errors right.

Below: Cleaning up the underside of a plinth using a smoothing plane

How do you know when to clean up each part – before or after gluing? The simple rule of thumb is to clean up and sand all internal faces, such as the inside of a drawer, prior to gluing. This allows you to deal with tight corners. You can clean up and sand external surfaces later.

How to Clean Up a Simple Frame

To clean up door stiles (end grain), work to an accurately marked knife line. Hold the work in a vice and plane inwards towards the rest of the door. This will stop the fibres of the wood spelching out (see page 74).

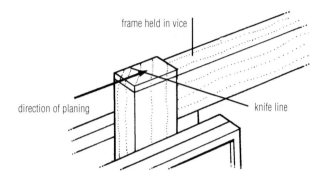

To clean up a bookcase shelf or rail that stands proud, work inwards, which will give the plane more control and stop it damaging the bookcase side.

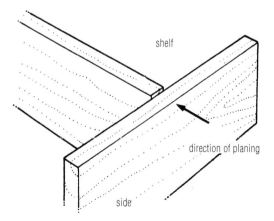

Sometimes you may have no choice but to clean up by planing in a direction that is not the most suitable, especially if the grain is tearing up badly. If so, take extra care, ensure the plane is sharp and remove only one shaving at a time.

How to Clean Up a Top Edge

To clean up constructions that are jointed at right angles, slide the plane around at 45 degrees to create a slicing action. This will prevent damage to the pieces of wood you are not planing and will produce a better cut. When making up drawers, if you can, select the wood for the sides so you plane from the front to the back of the drawer. This will stop you damaging the top edge of the front by planing across it.

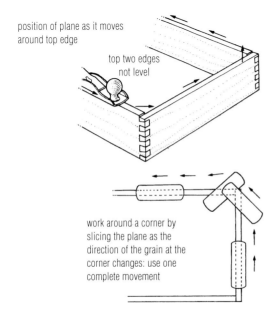

position of plane as it moves around top edge

top two edges not level

work around a corner by slicing the plane as the direction of the grain at the corner changes: use one complete movement

Cleaning up the surface of the frame

Take care with cleaning up. If you try to speed up the process, especially by planing across the grain on frames, the damage will be seen when you come to polish.

After planing, check the surface again and remove any torn grain with a cabinet scraper only if essential. Now you are ready to sand.

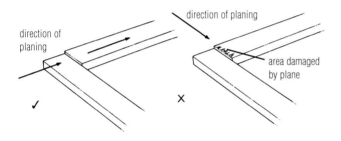

direction of planing

direction of planing

area damaged by plane

✓ ✗

How to Clean Up Dovetail Joints

Hold the dovetail joint securely in a vice. If there are any gaps in the joint repair them before cleaning up by filling them with a mix of very fine wood dust and glue. Use a sharp, finely set, smoothing plane to work the surface. Always plane towards the main body of the drawer or box. If the wood is particularly hard or difficult, you can use the plane in a circular motion to slice the wood, which will stop any grain from tearing out.

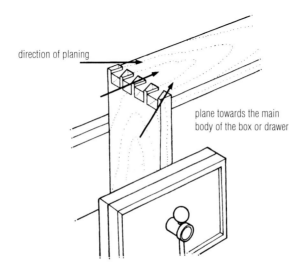

direction of planing

plane towards the main body of the box or drawer

How to Clean Up Edge Jointed Boards

When edge jointed boards are removed from the clamps, there will always be some cleaning up to do. There may well be a slight ridge where the boards meet at the joint or a small amount of cupping may take place if the wood adjusts to new surroundings while you are working on the rest of the project. Dimensional changes might even be caused by changes in the weather, especially during periods of extreme heat or damp (see page 9). This problem can be remedied with a smoothing plane. If there is any torn grain produced during planing, remove this using a cabinet scraper.

When you have checked the panel for being flat using a straight edge (see page 71), trim to size.

Finally, prepare the edges ready to accept any mouldings and then sand ready for finishing.

(see page 9)
(see page 71)

TIP

If PVA adhesive is allowed to dry on bare wood, a pale or white marking will appear during subsequent polishing. If it is possible sand the wood and apply two coats of polish/sealer before gluing so that you can easily wipe off the glue with a damp cloth. The faint grey markings left on the surface will instantly disappear on application of a further coat of polish. You can also try using an aliphatic PVA adhesive which, although expensive, leaves less noticeable glue marks.

GOOD ADVICE

Make sure that you always check the plane blade for sharpness and re-sharpen before starting to clean up. When working with tough woods such as oak it may be necessary to re-hone the plane blade at quite regular intervals to keep a keen edge.

TIP

If you see fine dust gathering in small pockets on the surface as you sand, this is an indication of damage or of a slight hollow. Check to see exactly why the dust is collecting, rather than just simply wiping it off.

TIP

Never plane work that has already been sanded – the blade will soon become blunt if you try.

TIP

Areas that are difficult to get to, such as the insides of small boxes, are best sanded and part-sealed before assembly. Ensure, though, that you do not get any polish on the joint as this will stop the glue bonding to the wood.

Right: Machine cutter marks show up as faint bruises under strong light. These stand out if not removed with a bench plane

Far right: Torn grain is caused where wood fibres have been pulled out. Remove using a cabinet scraper (see page 34)

SANDING

Sanding wood takes time. But without proper sanding it is impossible to achieve a professional finish.

Sanding removes the marks on the surface of wood caused by hand planing or scraping. The process is to use a coarse grit of abrasive paper to flatten the surface of the wood, and then to work through several grades of paper, getting finer each time, to remove any scratches left by the previous, coarser paper. Eventually, the scratches produced by sanding become so small that the eye cannot see them. It is only at this point that the wood is ready for polishing.

You will achieve more control when sanding by hand if you use a block (wrap a thin cloth around it if you wish) rather than your fingers. Never use an orbital sander on work that is to be polished as it will leave tiny circular scratches on the surface of the wood, totally ruining it.

How to Sand

Garnet paper is particularly suited to top quality work as it is kind to the wood. The grade of paper you start with depends on whether the wood is already quite smooth from the plane or not. For most furniture, start with 80 or 100 grit finishing paper, and then work through the grades – from around 150 to 240. On softwoods you can finish with 180 grade instead of 240, and on open-grained hardwoods, such as oak, you can finish with used 240 grade. There are more details on which grade to use on page 99.

If the surface is already quite smooth, do not start with a grade as coarse as 80 – instead use 120 or even 150 grade. It is important to let each grade do its fair share of the work. Beginners often have a tendency to work through the intermediate grades too quickly. A very fine paper will easily remove the marks left by a paper that is just a little more rough than itself, but it will never be able to remove the deep scratches left by a coarse one.

Always sand along the grain, never allowing the sanding block to sweep the surface in an arc and never let the paper clog up, as this will cause damage to the wood. Preparation of the surface is complete when all the defects have been removed, the wood is flat and it feels silky smooth to the touch. I cannot overstate the importance of sanding, especially on top quality work.

USING STOPPERS

TYPE OF STOPPER	HOW TO USE	DEFECT REPAIRED
Beaumontage: home-made blend of rosin (tree resin) and pure beeswax. Mix in equal parts (melt the rosin in a tin first) with a little pure turpentine and make into a stick	Soften a piece between fingers. Push into hole with screwdriver tip. Leave to dry. Clean off with a chisel, plane or sanding. Harder than wax filler sticks	For filling very small holes. Add colour using a little oil stain or pigment
Wax sticks: a proprietary blend of waxes	Use in the same way as beaumontage	For filling small holes and hair-line cracks
Shellac sticks: sold in a range of colours. The sticks are quite brittle and break easily	Melt a little of the stick into the hole with the end of a soldering iron. Use a chisel tip to press in and sand smooth	For repairing small holes or cracks before applying a high gloss finish e.g. French polish
Powder based stoppers: a mix of wood dust and powder made into a paste. Available in several colours or make by mixing PVA adhesive and fine wood dust	Select a suitable colour and fill the hole. Plane surface flat; then sand off. Like end grain they become darker when stained and polished	For use on small holes on lower quality work or where the defect will not be clearly visible

Note: Two-part wood rebuilders are recommended for repairing large holes and repairing missing wood

TIP

Always select a stopper which matches as closely as possible the final colour of the wood as most will not satisfactorily take a stain later.

After using a stopper you can use earth pigments to paint 'grain' or an artificial knot back on to the wood before polishing. This will help to conceal the defect.

Wood Stoppers

Wood stoppers are used to repair defects by filling holes and cracks. Do not confuse these with grain fillers, which are used to fill the pores of the wood prior to polishing (see page 103). Never use a stopper to fill torn grain. Although there are several types of stopper available, you can repair some defects without using them at all.

Defects that Do Not Require a Wood Stopper

Splits in New Wood

Splits in new wood are easily repaired and you can be sure the joint will be as strong as the wood itself. Put the wood in a vice and gently lean against it, opening up the crack. Squeeze PVA adhesive into the split and turn the wood around, leaning on it again to open it up from the other side. Squeeze glue into this side too. Next, use a vice, G-clamp or sash clamps to push the split tightly together. Wipe off any excess glue and leave it to dry. Finally, clean up this area of the wood with hand planes and sand.

Splits in Old Wood

If the wood is old and stable it is better to fill the split with a sliver of wood that will match the figure and appearance of the existing wood, rather than use a stopper. Any small gaps still left can be filled with coloured wax filler sticks, or beaumontage, and can even be painted out later if necessary.

Dents

If a dent has just been created on unpolished wood, lay a damp cloth on the dent, and using the tip of an electric iron, simply steam it out. As wood is made up of long, relatively hollow cells, steam puffs the crushed cells back out. It takes around 15–20 minutes for the dent to disappear – if the last little bit does not steam out, either plane the surface smooth again or fill the small hole with a stopper. Finally, sand the wood smooth.

Steaming out a dent (bare wood only). Wet area around dent with clean water. Press iron on damp cloth to steam out the defect. Repeat steaming for up to 20 minutes until dent is lifted out. Leave to dry. Resand, or replane and resand ready for finishing

dent

damp cloth

BEAUMONTAGE Genuine beaumontage, cabinet maker's stopper, is made by mixing equal parts of rosin (tree resin) with pure beeswax. Dilute slightly in pure turpentine and make into a stick. Melt the rosin first in a tin before adding the wax.

DENIBBING Rubbing down between coats of polish

ORBITAL SANDER Small pad sander that operates by oscillating in small circles. Leaves tiny scratches on the surface of wood which may stand out during polishing.

PAINTING OUT Using small amounts of pigment to mask a defect (e.g. to make a small hole look like a knot)

SPLITS Also known as shakes. Splits run along the grain. They are usually visible on both faces of a piece of wood. Ring shakes follow the line of the rings of the tree. Checks, also called surface checks, are very small splits visible on only one face

TYPES OF ABRASIVE PAPER

There are many abrasive papers suitable for sanding wood. The table opposite gives some idea of comparative grit sizes but remember that as some abrasives are softer they will blunt more quickly. In general woodwork the latter is a disadvantage, but there are times when it is actually an asset. Flour paper, for example, loses its cutting edge very easily (producing a much finer abrasive than the chart would seem to indicate), and is therefore excellent for wood finishing, being able to denib (rub down) softer polish without damaging its surface (see page 104).

Glass Paper
Tan or pale brown in colour, this is usually less expensive than most other abrasive papers. It blunts quickly during sanding. The finest grade is known as flour paper.

Garnet Paper
Made from industrial garnet crystals, which have the advantage of breaking while in use, constantly producing a new supply of cutting edges. Garnet paper is most suitable for hand sanding fine cabinet work.

Aluminium Oxide Paper
Generally mid brown to grey in colour, aluminium oxide is much tougher than garnet crystals, which makes them ideal for hand sanding very dense hardwoods and for use with sanding machines.

Self Lubricating Silicon Carbide Paper
A pale blue/grey paper, the most useful grades of which are 320 and 400 grit used in finishing. These are especially useful for denibbing polish as they cut extremely well and have a slightly lubricated feel, reducing scratch marks.

Wet ''N' Dry Paper
A dark grey silicon carbide paper, more often used in metalwork. Grades 600 to 1200 are sometimes used to denib tough varnishes and lacquers or for fine sanding.

Sanding Blocks
Sanding blocks are readily available in wood, cork or rubber or you can just as easily make your own from an offcut. The important thing to remember is that the block should be a little softer than the wood you are sanding, or it will damage the surface. Before using a block make sure that its face is flat and smooth.

If you use a cork block or a very soft rubber one, take care to ensure that it does not round over the edges you are sanding instead of keeping them square and crisp. One final word of warning, when sanding edges, look out for those long, needle-sharp splinters. It really does hurt if one happens to pierce its way through the paper into your hand!

1 Garnet paper
2 Aluminium oxide paper
3 Glass paper
4 Silicon carbide paper

COMPARATIVE GRADES OF ABRASIVE PAPERS

GLASS PAPER	GARNET PAPER	ALUMINIUM OXIDE PAPER	SILICON CARBIDE PAPER
Blunts easily	Suitable for hand sanding	Suitable for woodworking machinery and hand sanding	Finer grades up to 1200 grit are used to denib lacquer and surface coatings
		400	400*
	9/0 or 320	320	320*
	8/0 or 280	280	280
00 or flour*	7/0 or 240	240	240
0	6/0 or 220	220	220
	5/0 or 180	180	180
1	4/0 or 150	150	150
1½	3/0 or 120	120	120
F2	2/0 or 100	100	100
	0 or 80	80	80

* Suitable for denibbing
Note: very coarse grades of paper have been omitted from the chart

FINISHING

Above: Using a polishing mop to apply thin coats of French polish

Wood finishing seems an incredibly complex subject, but it can be surprisingly simple too. It is easy to achieve a professional-looking finish as long as you know what to do, and in what order to do it.

One of the challenges in finishing is knowing which products are compatible – i.e. which stain goes with which polish. Get it wrong and the result can be disastrous, and you may even have to start again. The information below gives black-and-white guidelines, but of course, there are always exceptions to any rules, so if you have even the slightest doubt, make sure that you consult your supplier.

What Stains and Polishes are Based On

Most stains and polishes suitable for home woodwork use will dilute in one of these three bases:

- Water
- Spirit (methylated spirit – denatured alcohol)
- Oil (derived from petroleum – hydrocarbons)

Industrial products, such as cellulose lacquer are much more specialized, and are not included here.

How to Decide What to Use

If you choose a traditional (wood dye) stain with a similar base to the polish you want to use, the two will try to blend together, and the most probable result will be a patchy finish. At the very least, the polish will become contaminated with the colour of the stain. Select a stain with a different base to that of the polish. That way the polish will seal the stain in and protect the wood.

Traditional Stains

Traditional stains are used to colour woods. This could be to enhance the grain, change the colour of the wood (perhaps to match another, more expensive, wood), or to make new furniture blend into existing surroundings. Traditional stains do not protect the wood. Some modern, coloured varnishes are confusingly called wood stains.

Polishes

Polishes seal the wood, protecting the surface, stopping it becoming soiled or finger-marked. Polishes reveal and enhance the figure and beauty of wood. Some polishes, such as French polish can, in practised hands, produce an incredibly high decorative shine. Generally, you need to select a polish that you feel will offer the best combination of protection and sheen.

HOW TO POLISH

Houses are built on foundations that are level and properly constructed; similarly, in wood finishing, the wood must be flat (with any defects repaired and holes stopped) and sanded smooth before staining and polishing begins.

What to Use

Oil finishes and wax polishes are easy to work with (two coats of sanding sealer before waxing will protect against finger-marking); French polish can be used to produce a decorative sheen/high gloss or if more protection to the surface is required, use a varnish.

The Process

The basic rules of finishing are to polish, denib and then clean.

1 Polish Apply a thin, even coat of polish, allowing it to dry properly in-between coats.

2 Denib Rub down the surface with fine abrasives to flatten it.

3 Clean Remove any dust from the surface, using a clean cloth or a 'tack cloth' (a special sticky cloth used to collect dust). On bare wood you can use a rag damped with white spirit to clean the wood but you must allow this to dry before starting to polish.

The polishing process is essentially the same for most products, including French polish. For example, a polisher's rubber (a pad made of cotton wadding with an outer cotton layer) is designed to put on very thin layers of polish.

A

B

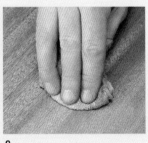
C

D

E

A Try not to lead on to the surface as this will cause the liquid polish to run down the edge. Instead, let the mop or brush glide off at the edges

B When the first coat of sanding sealer, French polish or varnish has dried, rub down (denib) with fine abrasive paper. If you use wire wool at this early stage, small particles will lodge in the pores of the wood

C Always remove the dust after denibbing each coat of polish.

D After the first two or three applications of polish (don't forget to rub down and clean off the surface between each one), you can move on to a finer abrasive. Here, 0000 grade wire wool is being used to denib the surface

E Finally, after cleaning the surface, apply wax polish with a soft cloth and leave for a few minutes to soak in. Buff off for a professional-looking natural sheen

Materials for basic finishing:
1 Soft mutton cloth for wax polishing
2 Paste wax
3 Polishing mop suspended in a jar of French polish
4 Dust removing cloth
5 Ultra fine 0000 grade wire wool
6 Polishing mop
7 Sanding block and fine abrasive paper

HOW-TO GUIDES

There are many finishing products, which offer different degrees of protection and shine. Each product has its own method of application, and the purpose of the following guides is to help you to produce a professional finish without first having to become a master polisher. Although the process is always to stain first and then polish, it is wise to select the polish first and then choose a stain, if you need one, that is compatible. You should always practise on scrap wood first, never on the real thing.

Oil Finishes

Oil Finishes – Penetrating Oils

Do not confuse oil finishes with petroleum-based, manufactured varnishes. Finishes such as tung oil, can occur quite naturally, although some oils may also contain chemicals to speed up the finishing process. Oil finishes are very easy to apply and offer some water resistance.

Oil finishes seal and protect the wood by first soaking into the surface and then hardening. Apply a reasonably liberal first coat and leave to soak in for 10–15 minutes or more, before wiping off the excess. Leave the rest of the oil to dry completely before buffing – this is crucial. The drying time for some proprietary brands of oil finish is 4–8 hours, but you will need to leave pure tung oil as long as 24 hours between coats. If you use raw linseed oil as a finish, thin it with pure turpentine (2 parts oil to 1 part turpentine) before use and leave for several days between applications.

After the first coat of oil has dried, apply further coats much more sparingly. You may like to rub the surface down between coats with 0000 wire wool to help flatten the oil and pull out the sheen. Always rub along the grain. Apply a minimum of three or four coats to produce a matt-satin sheen. Maintain the surface by re-oiling at regular yearly intervals or when required. For specific product information, read individual manufacturers' guidelines.

Note if the oil remains sticky on the surface, you may be applying it too thickly, or removing excess oil incorrectly.

Wax Polishes (Paste Waxes)

Wax polishes, like oil finishes, are easy, to use. Simple as they are, though, there are some pitfalls. There are two basic types of paste wax polish, those that go straight on to bare wood and those intended for previously sealed or polished surfaces – it is wise to choose the correct one.

Waxing Bare Wood

Apply the wax polish to the wood sparingly with a soft cloth so that it feeds and seals the surface as it soaks in. Leave it for 3–30 minutes or more after application, depending on the wax, until the surface is ready for buffing with a soft cloth.

It takes many coats of wax polish to build up a proper sheen, and the wax will require a great deal of buffing, which can be hard work. One problem is that if you apply the coats too thickly, the wax will build-up in corners and look unsightly.

Note: The above instructions are for paste wax polishes only. Liquid waxes are used for intricate surfaces such as old beams or doors. Do not use spray waxes on bare wood.

Waxing Sealed and Polished Wood

To speed up the waxing process, you can apply a sanding sealer to the wood first. Two or three coats of sanding sealer (or even white French polish, used as a sealer) will achieve a quick shine which will not become finger-marked (see Sanding Sealer). To speed up the process on pine furniture, you could apply the wax along the grain with 0000 wire wool, instead of a soft cloth, after the final coat of sealer. You must, however, use a soft cloth to buff the wax back off again.

1 White/clear paste wax
2 Coloured paste wax
3 Shellac sanding sealer
4 Penetrating oil (oil finish)
5 Coloured oil-based grain filler
6 Natural oil-based grain filler

You can make your own wax polish by simply mixing beeswax with pure turpentine, perhaps stiffening the mix a little with carnauba wax.

Sanding Sealer

Sanding sealer acts as a foundation for other polishes, which are applied on top of them. It is not a finish in its own right, but is extremely useful as a base for wax polish, French polish and some varnishes.

First make sure the wood is smooth, clear of dust and does not have any old finishes left on it. Apply each coat of sanding sealer with either a cotton cloth or a brush, ensuring that the sealer uniformly covers the surface of the wood. Leave it to dry and then denib along the grain (see page 105) with a fine abrasive paper, such as flour paper or 400 grit silicon carbide paper. Clean off the fine dust produced and apply another coat of sealer. Always denib between coats and keep the surface free of dust. Two or three coats of sanding sealer will generally be sufficient before proceeding to further polishing. Denib the last coat of sealer with 0000 grade ultra-fine wire wool instead of the flour paper if you prefer.

To create a simple finish using sanding sealer and wax polish:
1 Sand the wood and clean off dust.
2 Apply first coat of sanding sealer; denib; clean.
3 Apply second coat of sanding sealer; denib; clean.
4 Apply third coat of sanding sealer; denib; clean.
5 Apply paste wax polish, buffing off with a soft cloth.

French Polish / Modified French Polish

There is an easy and effective way to apply French polish using a brush or polisher's mop. (See note below on using a polisher's rubber.)

If applying French polish with a brush or mop, the secret is to thin the polish slightly in methylated spirit and use it as you would sanding sealer. However, you can apply many more coats than with the sanding sealer, building up the shine as you go. If you use this method, finish by denibbing the final coat with 0000 wire wool and apply a paste wax polish to protect the wood. The final result will be a very natural-looking, easily achieved, high shine on the wood, but not an extremely glossy 'piano finish'.

Different Colours

French polishes, as well as being clear, are also available in different colours. At times these are useful for adding tone to wood without having to mix up special polishes of your own (see page 107).

Note the secret to French polishing successfully with a rubber is to apply many very thin coats, working all of the surface to push the polish deep into the pores of the wood. Because of this, French polishing using a rubber is a lengthy and complicated process (see page 158 for books that will help).

Grainfillers

Grainfillers (which should not be confused with wood stoppers – see page 97), body up the surface of wood by filling the pores before polishing. They are used as a foundation for French polish or where a higher shine is required. Grainfillers either consist of superfine plaster of Paris mixed with water, or are available as factory-produced oil-based products. In both cases you apply them across the grain with a coarse rag to push the filler deep into the pores of the wood. Before the filler has dried completely, wipe off any excess filler with a new piece of rag. Grainfillers are not necessary for simple, basic finishing but are useful in more advanced polishing.

Above: Your choice of finish should be determined by the amount of shine and durability required. French polish (left) and oil finish (right).

FRENCH POLISH Made by dissolving shellac in methylated spirits. Available in many colours: transparent, white (clear), button (yellow), orange (orange) and garnet (brown).

CARNAUBA WAX A hard natural wax, also known as Brazilian wax

POLISHING MOP Finishing tool used to apply much thinner coats than a paint brush. Not generally used to apply varnish

LINT-FREE COTTON CLOTH Fine, textured cotton cloth with no synthetic content

Varnishes and Lacquers

Varnishes are effectively clear paints. They offer very good protection to the surface of the wood without obscuring its figure.

Water-based varnishes, which are often described as acrylic varnishes, tend to look milky, and may leave the surface with a slightly cloudy appearance after drying. However, the advantage of water-based varnishes is that they offer good protection, are very quick-drying, non-flammable and, importantly, are safe to use.

Manufacturers can add a matting agent to a varnish, which determines whether the varnish produces a matt, satin or gloss finish. Varnishes differ in this respect from products such as French polish, where it is the number of coats applied to the surface of the wood that dictates the depth of shine. You can buy coloured varnishes, although be careful when applying these by brush or you may see brush strokes.

Varnishes offer much more protection than oil finishes, wax polishes or French polish, but they can make the wood look artificial.

Lacquers are similar to varnishes, producing a very decorative, glossy surface coating on internal woodwork. Modern spray lacquers have been developed to produce a very hard-wearing, quick-drying gloss finish, which is often an attempt to imitate the glossy 'piano finish' of French polish.

Denibbing

Denibbing is the name given to the process of rubbing down between coats of polish. After a coat of polish has dried, a slight unevenness is left on the surface. Denibbing flattens out this unevenness.

It is important during denibbing to rub along the grain and not across it or in an arc. In the early stages of polishing you can denib quite heavily, but do not rub so hard that you break through the polish you have already applied. Be especially careful if you have stained the wood first. You must cover the whole surface uniformly and the process is only complete when the nibs have been removed and the polish looks perfectly flat. Check this by inspecting the surface of the wood closely, looking for any areas which are more shiny. Denibbing is of great importance on any surface that will become a feature, such as a table top.

In the very early stages of denibbing use either 00 grade flour paper or 400 grit self-lubricating silicon carbide paper rather than 0000 wire wool, webbed pads or powder abrasives. Papers will not break up leaving unwanted foreign bodies in the pores of the wood, and if used with a sanding block will also keep the first layers of polish much flatter.

You can change to 0000 ultra-fine wire wool or fine webbed pads after the first few coats of polish have sealed the surface of the wood.

French polishes
1 Transparent
2 White
3 Button
4 Orange
5 Garnet

Varnish:
6 Polyurethane
7 Acrylic (solvent-free) water-based

Shellac flakes:
8 Blonde dewaxed (for transparent polish)
9 Button
10 Garnet

Materials for Denibbing

Some of the products listed below are not suitable for basic finishing. Follow each How-to Guide for best results.

00 Grade Flour Paper

Used for initial denibbing. As the abrasive particles blunt easily, rub on a scrap piece of wood first to produce a fine abrasive paper before starting to denib.

320 and 400 Grade Self-lubricating Silicon Carbide ('Lubrisil') Paper

Very fine cutting paper suitable for harder finishes e.g. varnish, as well as sanding sealers and French polish.

600 to 1200 Wet ''N' Dry Paper

Used for denibbing very hard polishes and lacquers. Wet ''n' dry paper may need lubricating with finishing oil to help it cut.

Micromesh Abrasives

Some surface coating may be denibbed using very fine abrasives to create high-gloss finishes. Products such as microfine or micromesh are available up to 10,000 grit.

0000 (Pronounced 'Four Nought') Wire Wool

Made up into a soft wire pad to rub down polished surfaces. It can sometimes give light coloured woods a pale grey tone.

Webbed Pads

Manufactured pads produced in specific grades as an alternative to wire wool. They have the advantage of not breaking up or clogging during use. Ideal on curved surfaces including carvings and turnings.

Pumice Powder

Pumice and rottenstone powder abrasives are used in either a cotton pouch called a 'pounce bag' (which is simply rubbed along the polished surface), or a French polishing rubber.

Burnishing Cream/Paste

Not specifically used for denibbing. They contain an extremely fine abrasive and are used to cut back potentially shiny surfaces such as cellulose lacquer and French polish, to produce a very high gloss. The surface being burnished must have a full polished finish.

WHAT TO USE WHEN APPLYING POLISHES

WHAT TO USE	POLISH	COMMENTS
Ultra fine '0000' grade wire wool	First coat of wax polish	Wire wool may damage the surface unless applied along the grain only or use wire wool first and then apply wax polish with a soft cloth
White cotton/soft cloth	Oil finishes, wax polish, sanding sealer	Wax polish should always be buffed off with a very soft cloth such as a mutton cloth
Polishing mop	Sanding sealer, French polish, modified French polish	Allows controlled thin coats of polish to be applied if used properly
Polisher's rubber	French polish	With practice, allows polish to be pushed into the pores of the wood, building up a high shine
Brush	Varnish, French polish, sanding sealer	Brush strokes may remain visible as polish dries unless brushed in well
Flat lacquer brush	Varnish and some lacquers	A fine brush to apply thin coats of varnish
Specialist spray equipment	Lacquers	Industrial use: for repetitive polishing

TIP

LOOKING AFTER POLISHED FURNITURE

SCRATCH MARKS If the scratch has broken through the polished surface and bare wood is visible, apply a small amount of wood stain to the scratch to blend it in. Deeper scratches may need filling with coloured wax. Very fine scratches can be removed from surfaces that are not high gloss by lightly rubbing along the grain (covering the whole surface) with 0000 wire wool and antique wax.

WATER MARKS Often visible as a white bloom mark on the surface of the polish. If the water has penetrated the wood the surface may feel rough and repolishing may be necessary. If not, rub along the grain with 0000 wire wool and rewax. A little thinned raw linseed oil on the wire wool pad may help

RING MARKS For light markings only, abrade the surface gently and rewax (see water marks above)

REVIVING FURNITURE (prior to rewaxing) Older furniture may need rejuvenating to bring back its colour and sheen. Either use a proprietary brand of cleaner followed by a reviver, or make your own by mixing together one part raw linseed oil, one part white vinegar, one part methylated spirits and one part turpentine. Test on a small area first.

TIP

If you use powder stains to colour French polish add them to a little methylated spirits first, before introducing to the polish. This will help to distribute the stain evenly throughout the polish.

SAFETY

Some of the chemicals contained in wood stains may be dangerous. Always take suitable precautions.

HOW TO STAIN WOOD

You can alter the colour of wood using coloured finishes or traditional wood stains. As with polishes, there are also industrial types of stain, but these are not generally available in small quantities and for the sake of simplicity have not been included here. There are three main bases for wood stains:

- Water
- Methylated spirits – denatured alcohol (do not confuse with white spirit)
- Oil (white spirit)

To lighten the colour of a traditional stain, find out what it contains and dilute it in its own base chemical.

Traditional Wood Stains

Spirit-based Stains
Available in powder form for preparing your own colours, or as a ready-made liquid stain. If you choose stains from the same manufacturer's range, each colour should be totally intermixable with the rest to produce a wide variety of new colours and shades. Spirit stains are best applied by cloth. Do not confuse methylated spirits with white spirit, which is used in conjunction with oil-based stains.

Oil-based Stains
You can easily identify an oil-based stain because it will dilute in white spirit. Oil-based stains are the easiest wood stains to use and do not raise the grain of the wood. Apply by cloth or by brush. If you do use a brush, remove the

excess stain before it has dried with a lint-free cotton cloth. Oil-based stains are not usually light-fast and are therefore not suitable for antique restoration work.

Make sure that before you apply any polish to the wood, the oil stain is quite dry. This takes around 24 hours. If after this time the stain is still sticky, you have either applied too much or have not wiped it off correctly.

Water-based Stains
Water-based stains will sit beneath most polishes. They are usually light-fast, producing deep, subtle colours and have the advantage of safety, since they are not flammable.

Water-based stains are available in powder form as well as liquids and you can easily mix up your own colours. They are best applied by brush. Wipe off the excess stain after a

Top right: When staining always keep a live/wet edge as you work across a surface

A Apply stain along the grain with lint free cotton cloth

B Or, apply a thicker coat of stain to the surface with a brush. Do not let the stain dry out. Wipe off along the grain with a lint-free cotton cloth

A

B

RAISING THE GRAIN

Wood, as we know, swells as it absorbs moisture. If you apply any water-based product to a newly sanded surface, the fibres expand and the surface becomes quite rough again. The liquid content of water-based stains and varnishes always produces this effect on wood, and it is difficult to rectify after staining by sanding the surface.

To overcome this problem you must first raise the grain yourself. Sand the work smooth and then wet the wood with clean, warm water, using a cloth. Next, leave the wood to dry. You will now be able to feel the grain as bumps and ridges on the surface. Next re-sand, using a fine grade of abrasive paper (do not over-sand) – this will flatten the fibres again. Clean off any dust and then stain the wood. The grain will now not lift during staining.

few seconds with a clean lint-free cotton cloth. The one major disadvantage of water stains is that, as with all water based products, they raise the grain of the wood. To overcome this you must raise the grain first, before staining.

Natural Stains and Chemical Stains

Some stains are produced from natural products and others react with the wood to create a new colour. Vandyke crystals are one of the most popular traditional stains. These are made from walnut shells, and produce subtle brown colours, especially useful on oak. Dilute the flakes in hot water to create desired shade and strain off residue. Use Vandyke crystals as you would a water-based stain.

Chemical Stains
These are chemicals that genuinely stain wood rather than just dyeing it, by reacting with chemicals in the wood itself, which in turn creates a deep colour or shade. There are dozens of old recipes for chemical stains and certain woods such as oak, mahogany and walnut readily lend themselves to this type of staining. The depth of colour produced depends on the strength and size of the reaction and because of this, components such as rails may require colour toning to make them match the rest of the piece.

One bonus with chemical stains is that if you select two woods, one that reacts with the chemical stain and one that does not, you can create good contrasts between the two, which is especially useful on inlaid work.

Colour Toning

If you have stained the wood first to colour it, and have then started polishing, it is unwise to try to alter the colour any more with wood stains, as they will not penetrate the wood but sit on top of the polish. The finishing process is always stain first, polish second. But there are times when you may need to darken an odd rail or a panel that you have started to polish. To blend this in with the rest of the piece you will need to colour tone.

How to Colour Tone
Colour the polish, first using a compatible wood stain. For example, polyurethane varnish (oil-based) will be coloured easily by an oil-stain (i.e. those which will dilute in white spirit); whereas French polish (spirit-based) will be coloured by spirit stains or powders (which dissolve in methylated spirits).

Apply a lightly coloured polish to the component you want to tone, instead of the clear polish being used for the rest of the work. Do not let it colour any of the adjoining woodwork. Colour toning is, in effect, the application of coloured layers of polish, enabling one piece of wood to be blended in with the rest. Always colour tone with the same type of polish you are using for the rest of the work.

When you have colour toned the component sufficiently, revert to the clear polish you are using for the rest of the project. Be careful not to make the colour toned area shinier than the rest by applying more polish to it than the surrounding work.

PROJECTS

The six projects on the following pages bring together the information in the Tools and Techniques sections. They have been specially designed to show clearly how to work through the stages of constructing a piece of furniture. A list of essential skills can be found at the beginning of each project. Some techniques feature as special skills, but only when they are covered in detail (with illustrations and advice) within a particular project. If the same skill is necessary for making one of the other pieces of furniture, it is simply included in the list of basic skills.

Each project has step-by-step instructions, illustrations and photographs. Working drawings show how the piece of furniture fits together, and cutting lists tell you exactly what wood you need.

Always remember to number each piece of wood, and the parts of each joint, so that you can easily identify the components.

The projects progress from relatively simple to more difficult, and to build up your skills and knowledge it is best to read through them in order. To provide extra help all techniques are carefully cross-referenced. Before you start any project, read all the instructions (the information on using the working drawings and cutting lists on page 110 applies for all six projects). Try to visualize it at each stage of construction: the initial design; preparing the stock; marking and cutting out the carcase; making or fitting any embellishments and mouldings; and finally, sanding, gluing up and finishing.

HOW TO USE THIS SECTION

WORKING DRAWINGS AND CUTTING LIST

The drawings and cutting lists should be used in conjunction with the step-by-step instructions for each project.

The Working Drawings

Hatched Areas
Pieces of wood, or components that are shown in section (i.e., sliced through).

Dotted Lines
Show outlines and positions of components such as joints or rails that are important but would not normally be visible.

Centre Lines
(one short dash and one long one) Show where the centre of a cylindrical object (such as a turning) or where a component is symmetrical (i.e., in two mirrored halves). For

clarity, individual screws may not be shown but their position will be marked using centre lines.

Scales

The original drawings were prepared to scale, but because of a reduction in their size, and because of slight distortions that may occur during printing, these scales are not reproduced here. Instead, the drawings have been fully dimensioned to help you work more easily.

Details

Specific mouldings or profiles which may be small and unclear on the working drawing have been enlarged and are shown separately.

Cutting Lists

The cutting lists identify all the pieces of wood you need to make the furniture. They play an important part in outlining how each project is made. You should never order the wood for a piece of furniture without first understanding where each piece goes. You can check this by following the step-by-step instructions, the photographs and the drawings.

WOODWORK BENCH

The workbench is probably your most important tool. Having a solid, flat area at the right height will instantly improve the overall quality of your woodwork, helping you to gain control of the tools. This particular bench is made from white beech, the weight of which will stop it moving around the workshop while you are planing and sanding.

BASIC SKILLS

FITTING COMPONENTS USING WOOD SCREWS	53
MARKING OUT	64
PLANING BOARDS FLAT	70
EDGE-JOINTING BOARDS	79
CUTTING AND FITTING MORTISE AND TENON JOINTS	80
CUTTING AND FITTING HALVING JOINTS	83
GLUING UP	90
SANDING	96
BASIC FINISHING	100

HOW TO MAKE THE WORKBENCH STEP-BY-STEP

1 Preparing the Wood
Start by planing the wood straight and square (see page 70). When you have done this you can start work on the underframe.

2 Making the Underframe
This is made up from simple joints, but being large, they are a little on the heavy side to cut. The underframe carcase consists of two separate end frames, each having two rails. You need to fix these into the legs using mortise and tenon joints.

The bench is designed to be taken down and reassembled as required. Therefore, the only time you will use glue in the construction (except for the top itself) is during the assembly of these end frames.

Before gluing the end frames together it is important to mark out and cut the halving joints for the front and back rails. There are two at the back and one at the front (three in total).

Joint the two bottom rails into the legs using dovetailed halving joints, which give more rigidity (see page 69). Mark on the angle of the dovetail using a sliding bevel. Cut the dovetailed parts of the joint first and use these as a template.

Use straightforward through halving joints on the top back rail (see page 83).

When you have cut out the joints and checked them for fit, sand the legs and rails and glue up the end frames, checking for square.

3 Fitting the Top and Bottom Rails
When the end frames are properly dry, fit the single front rail and the two back rails using wood screws (do not use wood glue). It will help if you hold the entire frame in sash clamps, pulling the joints tight together. Drill pilot and clearance holes and insert the screws before removing the clamps (see page 53). Clean up the ends of the halving joints with a smoothing plane.

Above: Dovetail halving joints being screwed into position.

TIP

A bench should have a good clear area all around the underside of the top, allowing you unrestricted use of G-clamps and other holding devices.

TIP

The open ends of the tool well are cleaned out easily with a small dustpan and brush.

Right: Tool well bottom and spacers in place. Note the slots which will allow for the expansion and contraction of the top

Below: Underside of bench showing fixings for top. Note screw at back and slot to allow for expansion and contraction

4 Making the Tool Well

The tool well is simple to construct, being made up of just two lengths of wood, one wider than the other (see the cutting list). Use screws to fasten the wider of the two to the back rail and top edge of both end frames (the bench top forms the front of the tool well). Screw the narrower piece of wood into the first one, from the back, and at 90 degrees to it. It can also be screwed into the end frames and top back rail.

5 Fitting the Spacers for the Top

To allow the bench top to lie flat with the back of the tool well, you will need to screw two spacers to the top of the end frames to pack out the top. You should not glue any of these pieces in place, so it is of paramount importance that the screw fixings are good.

The spacers have a series of slotted holes, allowing you to hold the bench top in place from underneath. This permits the top to move if it needs to as a result of any changes in the moisture content of the atmosphere. Chamfer the fronts of the spacers in order to remove the sharp edges.

6 Making the Tool Rack

The tool rack at the back consists of one length of wood separated from the back of the tool well by small infill pieces of wood. These provide a gap into which the tools fit. Screw these into place. You can make the lower series of screws longer so that they fit right through the back of the tool well too. This makes for a much neater job.

7 Making the Bench Top

The bench top is made up of four pieces of 50mm (2in) thick beech, edge-jointed and glued together. Follow the instructions on page 79 for preparing wide panels and tops. This particular bench has also had two end pieces fitted after the top was planed flat. However, you should fit these to a bench only if the workshop that the bench is going into has a reasonably constant temperature and humidity. If you have a garage workshop where the moisture content of the atmosphere varies widely, it is wiser to leave off the end pieces, as they may cause the top to split later.

If you do fit the end pieces, it is important to plane the ends of the top carefully so that the glue has a good surface to bond to. Fit the bench top to the underframe through the spacers (see instruction 5).

8 Finishing

Generally speaking there is no need to finish a workbench to the same standard as you would furniture, although a sealer coat of varnish is helpful to protect against spillages. If you do apply varnish as a sealer, rub the entire bench down between coats with either 400 grade silicon carbide paper or 0000 wire wool, to flatten the nibs on the polish (see page 104). Thin the varnish slightly to help keep it flatter and make it easier to apply.

CUTTING LIST

COMPONENT	NUMBER	LENGTH	WIDTH	THICKNESS	COMMENTS
Top	1	1520mm (60in)	580mm (22¾in)	42mm (1⅝–1¾in)	Made up of 4 pieces edge-jointed together
length includes 2 end pieces 90mm (3½in) wide					
Tool well bottom	1	1520mm (60in)	180mm (7in)	20mm (¾in)	
Top supports	2	510mm (20in)	100mm (4in)	20mm (¾in)	
Tool well back	1	1520mm (60in)	105mm (4⅛in)	15mm (⅝in)	
Tool rack	1	1520mm (60in)	72mm (2⅞in)	15mm (⅝in)	
Tool well spacers	4	72mm (2⅞in)	72mm (2⅞in)	15mm (⅝in)	
Legs	4	820mm (32¼in)	95mm (3¾in)	70mm (2¾in)	
End frame rails	4	521mm (20½in)	75mm (3in)	40mm (1⅝in)	Including tenons
Back top rail	1	1170mm (46¼in)	140mm (5½in)	40mm (1⅝in)	
Front and back bottom rails	2	1170mm (46¼in)	130mm (5⅛in)	40mm (1⅝in)	

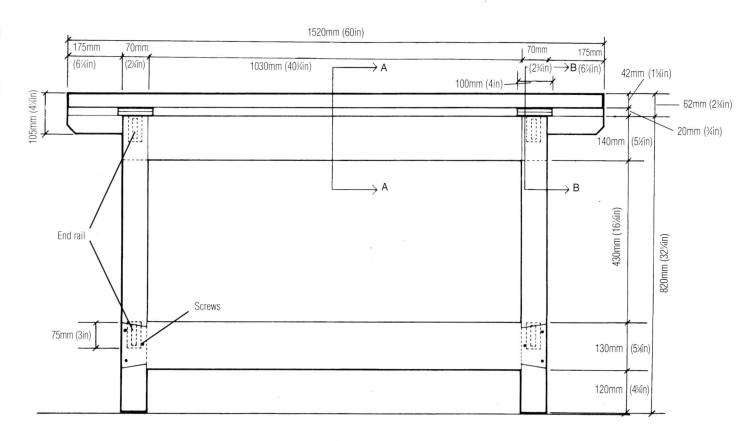

1520mm (60in)

175mm (6⅞in) 70mm (2¾in) 1030mm (40¾in) →A 100mm (4in) 70mm (2¾in) →B (6⅞in) 175mm

42mm (1⅝in)

62mm (2⅜in)

20mm (¾in)

105mm (4⅛in)

140mm (5½in)

A → A

B → B

430mm (16⅞in)

820mm (32¼in)

End rail

Screws

75mm (3in)

130mm (5⅛in)

120mm (4¾in)

FRONT ELEVATION

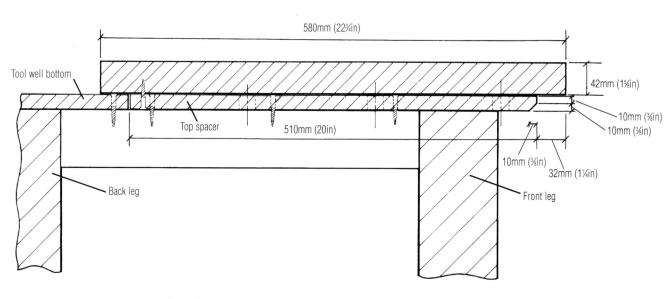

580mm (22¾in)

Tool well bottom

42mm (1⅝in)

10mm (⅜in)

10mm (⅜in)

Top spacer

510mm (20in)

10mm (⅜in)

32mm (1¼in)

Back leg

Front leg

SECTION THROUGH FRONT OF BENCH B – B

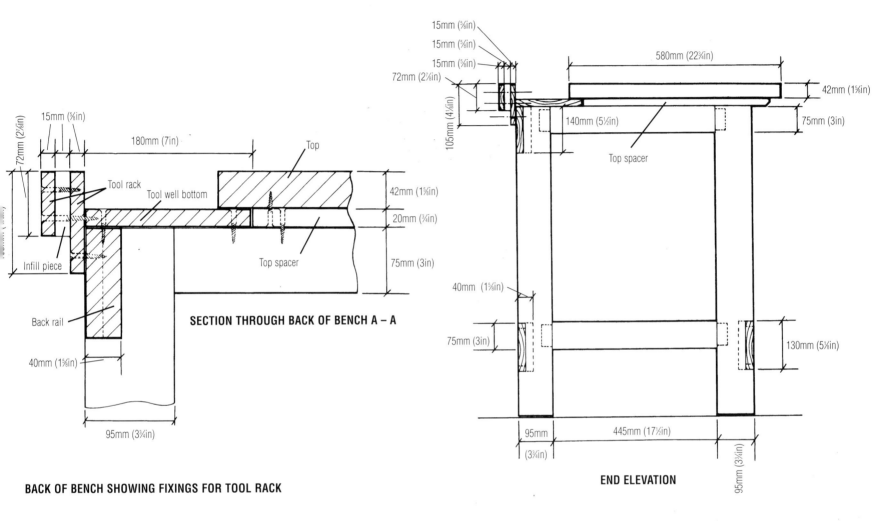

SECTION THROUGH BACK OF BENCH A – A

15mm (⅝in)

72mm (2⅞in)

180mm (7in)

Top

Tool rack

Tool well bottom

Top spacer

42mm (1⅝in)

20mm (¾in)

75mm (3in)

Infill piece

Back rail

40mm (1⅝in)

95mm (3¾in)

15mm (⅝in)

15mm (⅝in)

15mm (⅝in)

72mm (2⅞in)

105mm (4⅛in)

580mm (22¾in)

42mm (1⅝in)

140mm (5½in)

75mm (3in)

Top spacer

40mm (1⅝in)

75mm (3in)

95mm (3¾in)

445mm (17½in)

95mm (3¾in)

130mm (5⅛in)

END ELEVATION

BACK OF BENCH SHOWING FIXINGS FOR TOOL RACK

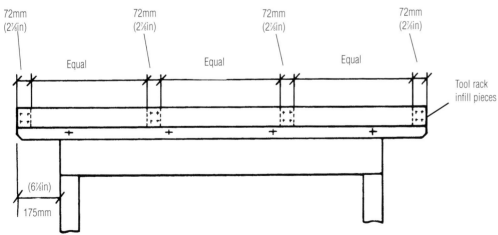

72mm (2⅞in)

72mm (2⅞in)

72mm (2⅞in)

72mm (2⅞in)

Equal

Equal

Equal

Tool rack infill pieces

(6⅞in)

175mm

BOOKCASE

This bookcase is constructed in pine, which is a soft material when compared with dense timbers such as oak. It is an easy timber to work with and finish.

BASIC SKILLS

USING A COPING SAW	29
MARKING OUT	64
PLANING BOARDS FLAT	70
MOULDING EDGES	75
CUTTING AND FITTING MITRES	77
EDGE-JOINTING BOARDS	79
CUTTING AND FITTING MORTISE AND TENON JOINTS	80
CUTTING AND FITTING HALVING JOINTS	83
CUTTING AND FITTING BAREFACED HOUSING JOINTS	85
GLUING UP	90
SANDING	96
BASIC FINISHING	100

SPECIAL TECHNIQUE

FITTING A TOP	121

HOW TO MAKE THE BOOKCASE STEP-BY-STEP

1 Edge-jointing and Planing the Wide Boards

The sides, top, bottom and shelves of the bookcase are each jointed up from two pieces of wood, edge-jointed together and planed flat (see page 71 and 79). Once you have jointed them up, allowing extra for trimming to size, you need to prepare them ready for marking and cutting the joints.

2 The Carcase

The bookcase carcase consists of two solid sides, two shelves and a bottom. It has a back constructed of bead and butt boarding, which is a ready-bought wooden cladding with a bead running down one edge. This is held in a rebate on the back rails and sides. There is also a moulded top front rail which will prevent the top front edges of the sides from cupping outwards. This rail will also provide a fixing point for the top.

All these separate components make up the main body of the bookcase, and should be made first, before the top and the plinth.

3 Making the Carcase

The main joints used for the carcase are stopped barefaced housing joints (see page 85) and these hold the shelves and bottom in place. Mark the positions of the joints and clearly show the waste.

The front rails of the carcase will be held in place with stub tenons (see page 80): mark their positions.

The top and bottom rails at the back are held in place with halving joints: you should mark the shoulder lines of all these components at this stage to guarantee that all shelves and rails match each other in length.

Next cut and fit the joints.

4 Moulding the Edges

First cut out any curved edges using a coping saw and then clean them up before moulding (see page 29). Running down the two outside front edges of the sides and along the front edge of the base is a quirk bead. The edges of each shelf and the top front rail are ovolo moulded. These mouldings soften the edges, stop them being damaged and enhance the overall look of the piece. It is best to form these mouldings

Right: Bookcase plinth showing glue blocks and plinth supports

using a small electric router with a bearing bit, as a combination plane will have difficulty following the cut-out section of the top front rail.

5 Fitting the Back

You should now be left with the basic carcase for the bookcase. Glue the carcase together and cut the bead and butt boarding to length to fit into the rebates in the back rails and sides. (Hold the boarding in place with two thin cover strips and screw into position.) Use wood screws to fasten every second or third board to the shelves from behind, as this will keep the back rigid and will remove any slight gaps between them and the backs of the shelves. You may prefer to seal the wood prior to gluing (see page 101) to remove any chance of white glue markings appearing on the wood later. If so, make sure all the joints fit, so there is a minimum of cleaning up to do later.

6 Making and Fitting the Top

Once the cabinet work for the carcase is complete, trim the top to size, finishing off the edges with a smoothing plane. Round the front corners and then sand them ready for moulding. It is important that these edges are not left rough before putting on the ovolo mould, because any tool used for moulding will follow the slightest undulation on the edge and the finished result will look poor.

The top should overhang about 10mm (⅜in) at the back and about 15mm (⅝in) at the front and sides. Hold it in place with stretcher plates (see right). These will allow the top to expand or contract if it needs to.

7 Making the Plinth

The plinth is made up as a separate component from the carcase and is screwed in place through plinth supports from below. Use mitres at the two front corners (see page 77) and corner butt joints at the back (see page 79). Glue blocks strengthen the joints. The top front edge and both sides of the plinth have a decorative double ovolo mould – there is no need to continue this around the back edge. Cut out the front of the plinth with a coping saw so it matches the top rail of the bookcase carcase. It too has an ovolo moulding.

SPECIAL TECHNIQUES

FASTENING TOPS IN PLACE

rail

Method 1
using stretcher/ expansion plates

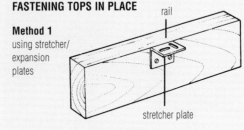
stretcher plate

if wood shrinks in this direction use this slot

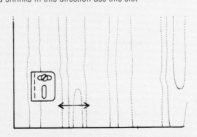

if it shrinks in the other direction use this slot

Method 2
using wooden buttons

screw hole

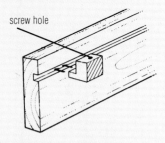

wooden button fits into groove on inside edge of rail and slides along it as top moves due to moisture changes

Below: Table stretcher plates in position. Note the bead and butt boarding

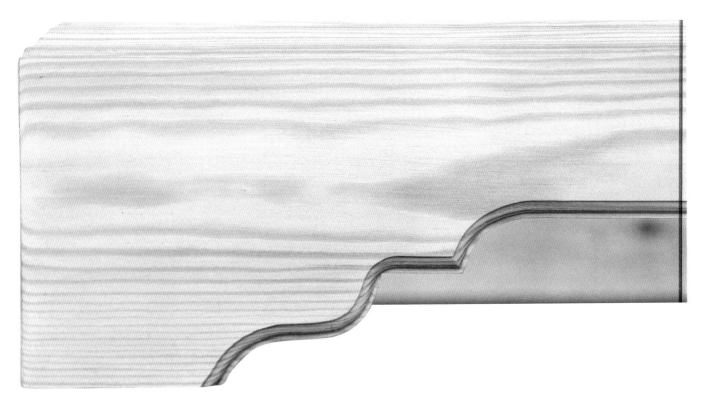

Above: Profile of bookcase plinth with single ovolo mould. Double ovolo mould on the top edge

Right: Take care when planing: remember, 10 plane shavings measure about 1mm (³⁄₆₄in)

8 Making the Decorative Cut-Out Mouldings

Mark the shape of the cut-outs on to the wood using a template made of thin card or hardboard. Mark the waste and cut it out using a coping saw: this way, the curves will not cause a problem, as the saw blade will easily be able to follow very tight bends.

After removing the waste, clean up the saw marks. I find that sharp broad chisels and round or half-round files produce an acceptable, smooth surface prior to moulding an edge.

9 Sanding

You can glue up the plinth prior to sanding if you wish as all external parts are easily accessible, but with the main carcase, it is better to sand each piece of wood first (especially internal faces) before gluing up. Start sanding on a coarse/medium grit of garnet paper, such as 80/100, and use intermediate papers (e.g. 120 and 150 grade) as necessary, finishing on 180 grade garnet paper (see page 96).

10 Finishing

Good choices of finish for a pine bookcase include an oil finish (see page 102); or sanding sealer and wax polish (see page 103); or French polish/modified French polish and wax, applied in the same way as sanding sealer (see page 103).

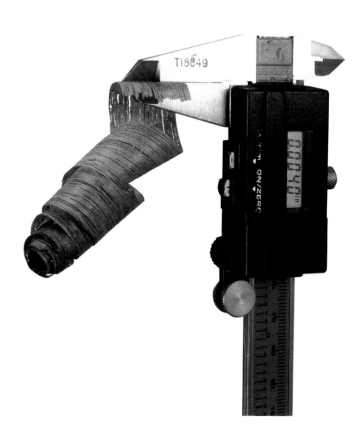

DECORATIVE EDGE MOULDINGS

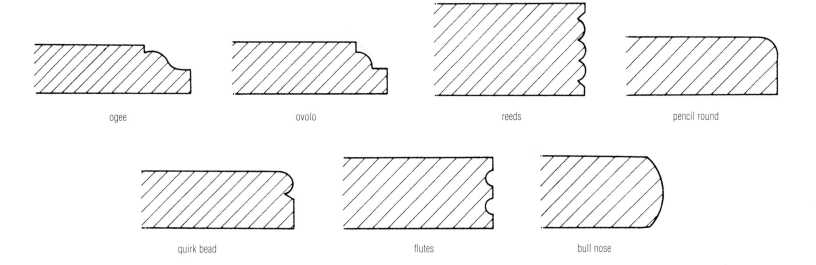

ogee ovolo reeds pencil round

quirk bead flutes bull nose

CUTTING LIST

COMPONENT	NUMBER	LENGTH	WIDTH	THICKNESS	COMMENTS
Top	1	800mm (31½in)	315mm (12½in)	20mm (¾in)	Jointed up in 2 pieces
Shelves	2	750mm (29½in)	261mm (10⅜in)	20mm (¾in)	Jointed up in 2 pieces
Base	1	750mm (29½in)	290mm (11½in)	20mm (¾in)	Jointed up in 2 pieces
Sides	2	895mm (35⅛in)	290mm (11½in)	20mm (¾in)	Jointed up in 2 pieces
Top back rail	1	750mm (29½in)	40mm (1½in)	20mm (¾in)	
Bottom back rail	1	750mm (29½in)	40mm (1½in)	20mm (¾in)	
Front top rail	1	750mm (29½in)	52mm (2in)	20mm (¾in)	
Bead and butt boarding made up of 10 pieces 14mm (½in) thick by 75mm (3in) lay measure					
Plinth – front	1	800mm (31½in)	95mm (3¾in)	20mm (¾in)	
Plinth – sides	2	310mm (12¼in)	95mm (3¾in)	20mm (¾in)	
Plinth – back	1	760mm (30in)	95mm (3¾in)	20mm (¾in)	
Back cover strips	2	755mm (29¾in)	35mm (1⅜in)	4mm (³⁄₁₆in)	
Glue blocks			20mm (¾in)	20mm (¾in)	From scrap
Plinth supports 2.4m (8ft)			20mm (¾in)	20mm (¾in)	

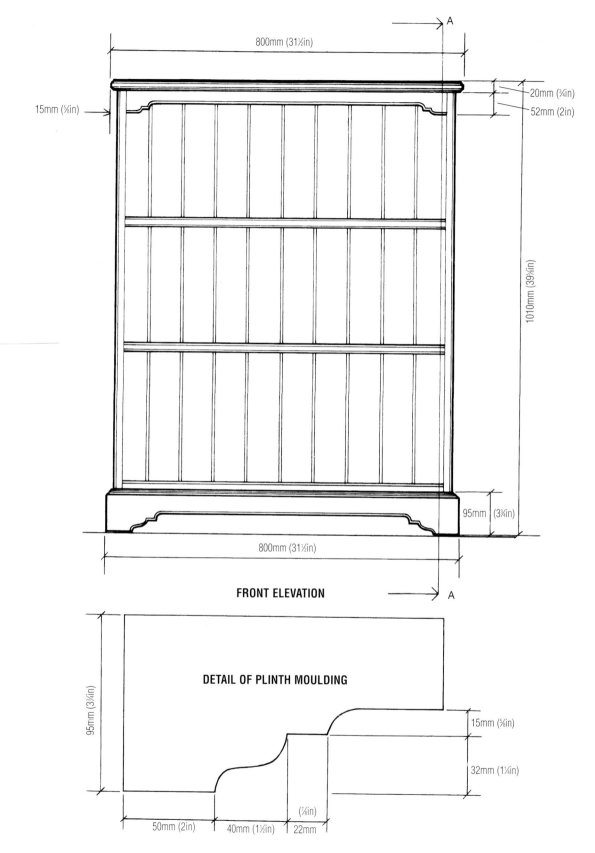

A

800mm (31½in)

15mm (⅝in)

20mm (¾in)

52mm (2in)

1010mm (39⅝in)

95mm (3¾in)

800mm (31½in)

FRONT ELEVATION

A

95mm (3¾in)

DETAIL OF PLINTH MOULDING

15mm (⅝in)

32mm (1¼in)

50mm (2in)

40mm (1½in)

22mm

(⅞in)

Bookcase

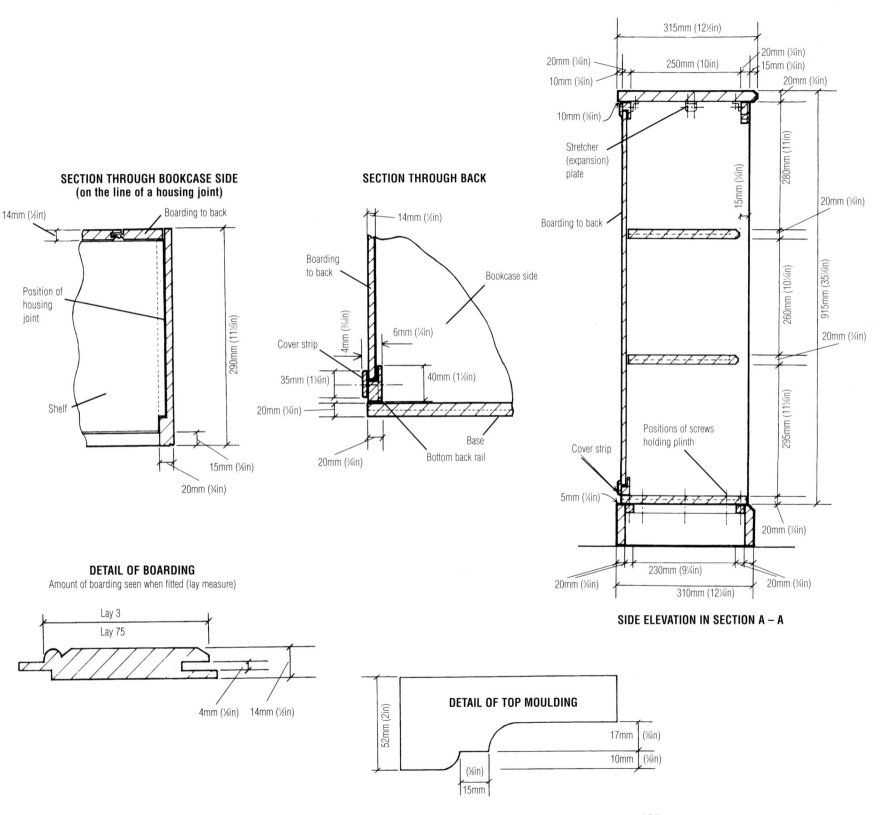

SECTION THROUGH BOOKCASE SIDE
(on the line of a housing joint)

14mm (½in)
Boarding to back
Position of housing joint
Shelf
290mm (11½in)
15mm (⅝in)
20mm (¾in)

SECTION THROUGH BACK

14mm (½in)
Boarding to back
Bookcase side
Cover strip
4mm (³⁄₁₆in)
6mm (¼in)
35mm (1⅜in)
40mm (1½in)
20mm (¾in)
20mm (¾in)
Bottom back rail
Base

315mm (12½in)
250mm (10in)
20mm (¾in)
15mm (⅝in)
20mm (¾in)
20mm (¾in)
10mm (⅜in)
10mm (⅜in)
Stretcher (expansion) plate
15mm (⅝in)
280mm (11in)
915mm (35⅞in)
Boarding to back
20mm (¾in)
260mm (10¼in)
20mm (¾in)
Cover strip
Positions of screws holding plinth
295mm (11⅝in)
5mm (¼in)
20mm (¾in)
20mm (¾in)
230mm (9¼in)
20mm (¾in)
310mm (12¼in)

SIDE ELEVATION IN SECTION A – A

DETAIL OF BOARDING
Amount of boarding seen when fitted (lay measure)

Lay 3
Lay 75
4mm (⅛in)
14mm (½in)

DETAIL OF TOP MOULDING

52mm (2in)
17mm (⅝in)
10mm (⅜in)
(⅝in)
15mm

CHILD'S DESK

All the ash veneered MDF required for this piece of furniture can be cut from one standard sheet measuring 2440 x 1220 x 19mm (96 x 48 x ¾in). The desk is suitable for a child aged 8–12 years.

BASIC SKILLS

CUTTING SHEET MATERIALS	9
MARKING OUT	64
CUTTING AND FITTING MITRES	77
CUTTING AND FITTING HOUSING JOINTS	84
MARKING OUT AND CUTTING DOVETAILS	85
GLUING UP	90
SANDING	96
BASIC FINISHING	100
FITTING HINGES	146
MAKING A DRAWER	154

SPECIAL TECHNIQUES

WORKING IN SHEET MATERIALS	129
GROOVING WOOD USING A COMBINATION PLANE	129

SHEET MATERIALS

All sheet materials have advantages and disadvantages. Here we have chosen MDF but you may decide to work instead in plywood or chipboard. These are some pros and cons to bear in mind.

	MDF*	PLYWOOD	CHIPBOARD
FOR	Produces good crisp edges and will take stains and polishes. Available with decorative veneers on both faces. Screws and glues easily	Stable board, easy to work	Economically priced sheet material, readily available
AGAINST	Difficult to work with hand tools. The grooves here are best formed with a small electric router or by lipping all edges and grooving these with a combination plane. Produces irritant dust so wear suitable protection when sanding	Not usually available as a decorative veneered board thicker than 12mm (½in)	Core of chipboard can be quite coarse causing difficulty with screws and glue. Difficult to work with hand tools. Traditional techniques can result in quite weak joints

*Medium Density Fibreboard

126

HOW TO MAKE THE DESK STEP-BY-STEP

1 Preparing the MDF (Medium Density Fibreboard)

First mark out each component on the full sheet of MDF in pencil (see cutting list, page 133). Allow for the width of your saw cut plus a little extra in case you wander from the line. When you are sawing sheet materials, there is a risk that the underside may spelch out, so take extra care. Once you have cut out each piece, square the edges accurately using hand planes (see page 73), and lip all important edges ready for jointing. This includes back edges too, especially if you are to use a combination plane to work the groove.

2 Making the Pedestal

The pedestal is the part of the desk containing the shelves. Join the two shelves and base to the sides using stopped, barefaced housing joints, which are strong and also give more rigidity to the carcase (see page 85). Form a 6mm (¼in) groove running down the back inside face of the sides, and along the base, to hold the plywood back. Make a small top back rail, also with a groove, to hold the plywood at the top. This slides into place after gluing the pedestal. Under the base there is a small plinth, which is housed in position. Mark out and cut all the joints for the pedestal before progressing on to the rest of the desk.

3 Creating the Kneehole

The area of desk where the child sits is called the kneehole. This is formed on one side by the pedestal, and on the other by a simple upright panel. Both sets of uprights – the pedestal and the panel – are housed into the top, and you must allow for this extra when working out the initial measurements. The small drawer slides on a single piece of ash veneered MDF, which is housed into place and provides extra rigidity and support for the upright panel. At the back of the kneehole is a gently curved back panel which is held in place using barefaced housing joints. This is fastened to the pedestal and to the single upright to create a stronger construction (see Special Techniques, page 129).

4 Making the Top

Make up the top in two parts. The lower part is fixed to the base with stopped housing joints (see page 84), while the upper part of the top is split into two and lipped where the two pieces meet. The left-hand side will later be hinged to create a drawing board which tilts into three positions. The fixed flat top at the right-hand side is ideal for making notes, storing papers or to hold an adjustable lamp for studying. This is held in place with wood glue and by screwing from underneath. Cut the recesses for the tilt positions of the top by carefully marking out and cutting with a chisel. Clean up with a router plane.

5 Making the Tilt Top Stays

There are two tilt top stays, each constructed of a single length of beech. Drill them at one end to hold a steel dowel. Hold this dowel in place in turn with two small pieces of beech, similarly drilled. Glue these to the recess in the underside of the drawing board.

Left: The plywood back being slid into position

IMPORTANT

To save money, the shelves, being hidden, can be made of either unveneered MDF, chipboard or plywood lipped to match the ash MDF at the front. These are not allowed for in the marking out of the full sheet of MDF.

TIP

To prevent sagging, always store sheet materials flat and never propped upright. Cut to size before storing if necessary.

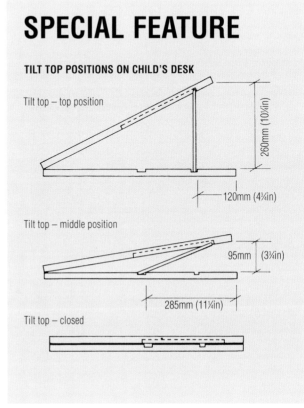

TILT TOP POSITIONS ON CHILD'S DESK

Tilt top – top position

260mm (10¼in)

120mm (4¾in)

Tilt top – middle position

95mm (3¾in)

285mm (11¼in)

Tilt top – closed

Above: Close-up view of tilt top stays

6 Gluing Up

After careful sanding, you can glue the pedestal, before sliding in the plywood back. Leave this to dry and then glue it to the single upright panel, the drawer support, the back panel, and the lower part of the top. This will create the complete carcase to which the drawing board can be fitted.

7 Making the Drawer

The drawer should really be considered as a shallow tray, although you still construct it using traditional drawer-making techniques (see page 104). It does not need any separate runners, kickers or guides as these are all taken care of by the carcase and top.

8 Fitting the Drawing Board

The left-hand upper part of the top forms the drawing board. Glue the tilt top stays into position first, before fitting a single pair of hinges at the front to provide a pivot point (see page 146 on fitting hinges). After fitting the drawing board, put the small fixed top into position. Check and plane the edges of this to create a good fit with the lower part of the top. Glue and screw it into place. Sand ready for finishing.

9 Finishing

A good, quick finish for this desk is to apply two or three coats of clear satin acrylic varnish. This should be rubbed down between coats (see page 105). Being coarse-textured, ash is best denibbed using a fine abrasive webbed pad or flour paper so that small particles do not become caught in the grain. To produce a silkier feel to the surface of the wood, you can rub the last coat of varnish down with the abrasive pad and apply a very small amount of clear paste wax, rubbed well in with a soft cloth.

SPECIAL TECHNIQUES

WORKING IN SHEET MATERIALS

We know that solid wood is prone to warping or splitting as it dries out or readjusts to new surroundings. This is why the secondary conditioning of solid wood is so important. Solid wood has another drawback in that to make up wide panels and tops, you need considerable time and some skill to edge-joint boards together and then accurately plane them smooth again. MDF, and other sheet materials provide an alternative, ready-made flat, stable base. As they can have a thin layer of decorative veneer glued to them already, all you have to do is simply cut out the shapes or profiles you need and assemble them using similar methods to flat-pack furniture.

However, it is not quite as simple as it sounds. When you are working with sheet materials, there are two very important considerations. The first is that it is vital to strengthen the construction.

If you take a cardboard box and try to push together two opposite corners of the box, the rigidity given by the bottom will stop the box folding up easily. If you take out the bottom of the box, the rigidity is lost. Therefore, when designing furniture in sheet materials, you must always strengthen the carcase, either by boxing in the back rigidly, or by using some form of triangular configuration across its corners to try to stiffen the framework.

On this child's desk, a plywood back is glued into grooves behind the shelves on the pedestal to add strength. A piece of MDF is also housed into the knee-hole area of the desk and is glued in place. This will offer much-needed support.

The second problem with working in sheet materials is that edges usually need lipping in some way – a real give-away for antique furniture lovers! You can use iron-on edgings but these tend to peel off or become damaged over quite a short period of time. On this desk, quite wide pieces of wood, around 12–30mm (½–1⅛in), have been used as edgings. This width allows for the edges to be easily cleaned up, moulded (or grooved) if necessary and polished. It also helps with any remoulding or repolishing if the edges are accidentally damaged during the lifetime of the furniture.

Apply wide edgings such as these using the same technique as edge-jointing boards (see page 79), planing the lipping to exact size later. Be careful not to spill glue on the veneer, or to damage the face veneer during planing.

GROOVING WOOD USING A COMBINATION PLANE

Start at one end, working from a face edge. Work an area around 380mm (15in) long until you reach the correct depth

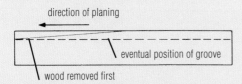

direction of planing

eventual position of groove

wood removed first

Slowly work back towards the other end making the groove longer as you go. Work short areas at a time

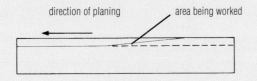

direction of planing   area being worked

Finish by pushing the combination/plough plane from one end of the groove to the other

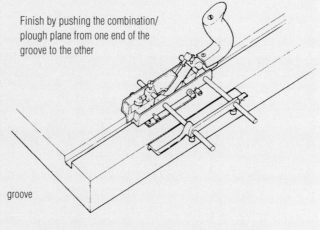

groove

Make sure that the fence of the plane is held firmly against the face edge

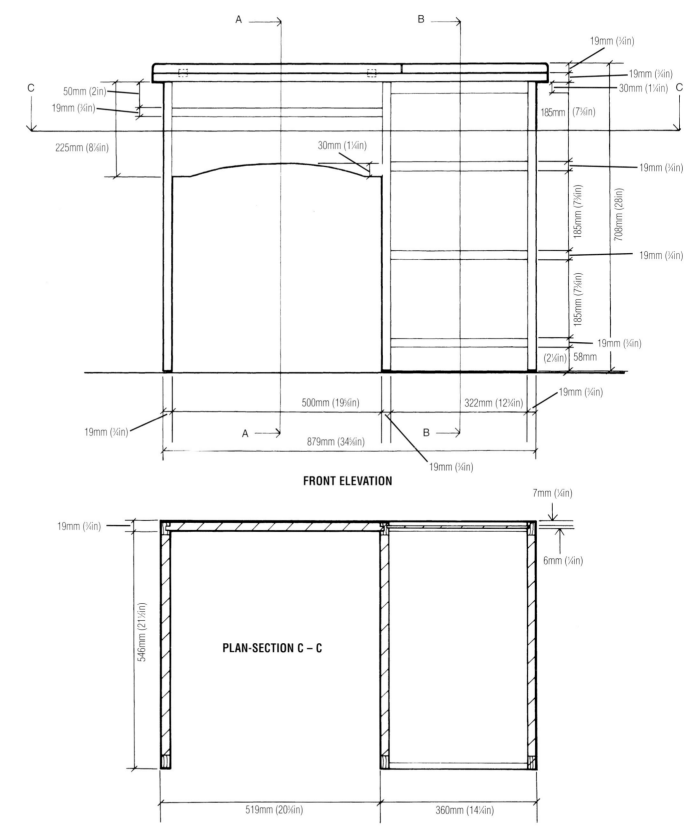

C

A →

B →

19mm (¾in)

50mm (2in)

19mm (¾in)

19mm (¾in)

19mm (¾in)

30mm (1¼in)

C

185mm (7⅜in)

225mm (8⅞in)

30mm (1¼in)

19mm (¾in)

185mm (7⅜in)

708mm (28in)

19mm (¾in)

185mm (7⅜in)

19mm (¾in)

(2⅛in) 58mm

19mm (¾in)

500mm (19⅝in)

322mm (12¾in)

19mm (¾in)

A →

B →

879mm (34⅝in)

19mm (¾in)

FRONT ELEVATION

7mm (¼in)

19mm (¾in)

6mm (¼in)

546mm (21½in)

PLAN-SECTION C – C

519mm (20⅜in)

360mm (14¼in)

130

SIDE ELEVATION A – A IN SECTION

mm (¾in)

225mm (8⅞in)

Kneehole back panel

565mm (22¼in)

SIDE ELEVATION B – B IN SECTION

19mm (¾in)

19mm (¾in)

30mm (1¼in)

25mm (1in)

155mm (6⅛in)

19mm (¾in)

708mm (28in)

185mm (7⅜in)

barefaced housing joints

19mm (¾in)

185mm (7⅜in)

19mm (¾in)

58mm (2¼in)

19mm (¾in)

25mm (1in)

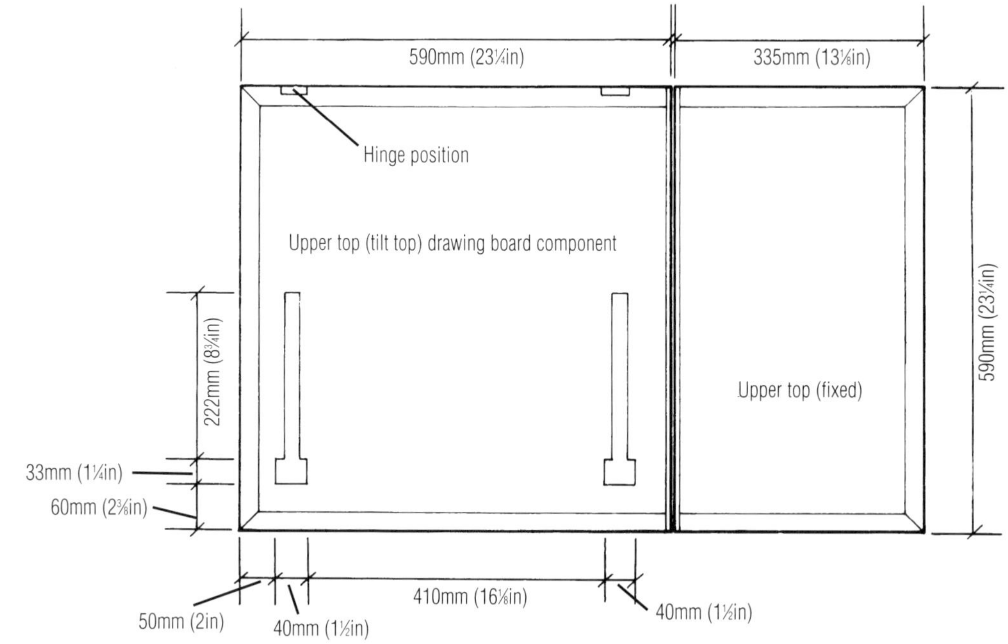
590mm (23¼in)
335mm (13⅛in)
Hinge position
Upper top (tilt top) drawing board component
222mm (8¾in)
33mm (1¼in)
60mm (2⅜in)
Upper top (fixed)
590mm (23¼in)
50mm (2in)
40mm (1½in)
410mm (16⅛in)
40mm (1½in)

DETAIL OF UNDERSIDE OF UPPER TOP SHOWING TILT TOP POSITIONS

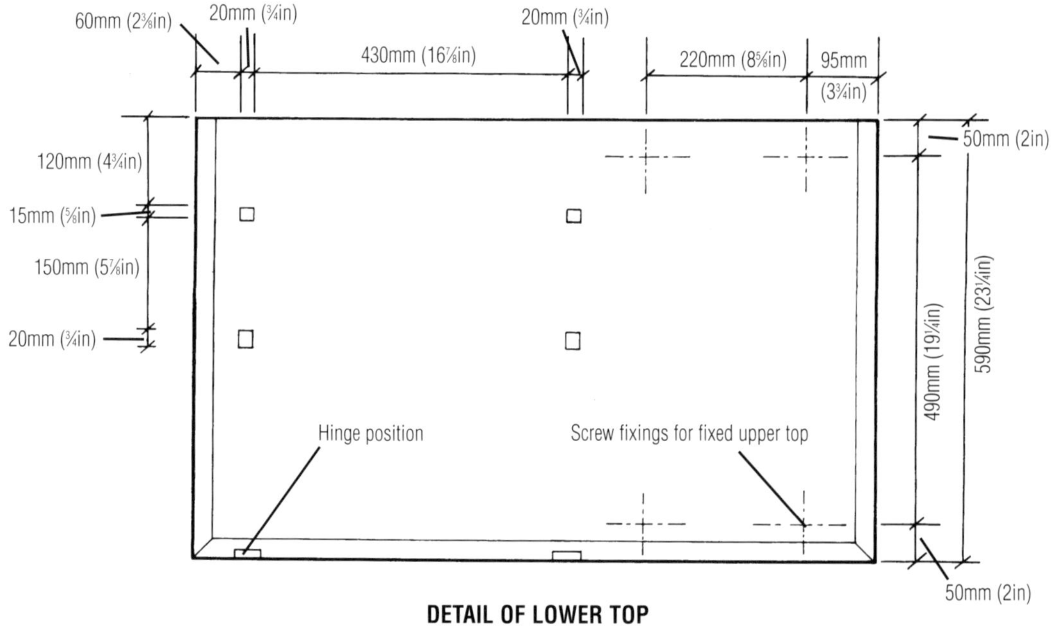
60mm (2⅜in)
20mm (¾in)
430mm (16⅞in)
20mm (¾in)
220mm (8⅝in)
95mm (3¾in)
50mm (2in)
120mm (4¾in)
15mm (⅝in)
150mm (5⅞in)
20mm (¾in)
Hinge position
Screw fixings for fixed upper top
490mm (19¼in)
590mm (23¼in)
50mm (2in)

DETAIL OF LOWER TOP

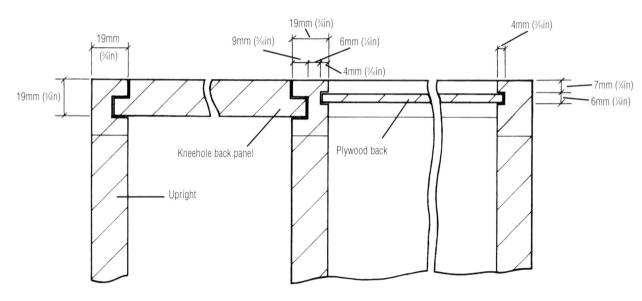

DETAIL IN PLAN – SECTION THROUGH KNEEHOLE AND PEDESTAL

CUTTING LIST

COMPONENT	NUMBER	LENGTH	WIDTH	THICKNESS	COMMENTS
One 2440 x 1220 x 19mm (96 x 48 x ¾in) sheet of ash veneered Medium Density Fibreboard cuts:	1				Note: Sizes shown are for each complete component. Deduct width of lippings before cutting MDF to size
Uprights	3	680mm (26⅞in)	565mm (22¼in)	19mm (¾in)	
Upper part of top	1	590mm (23¼in)	590mm (23¼in)	19mm (¾in)	
Upper part of top	1	335mm (13⅛in)	590mm (23¼in)	19mm (¾in)	
Lower part of top	1	925mm (36⅜in)	590mm (23¼in)	19mm (¾in)	
Drawer support	1	520mm (20⅜in)	546mm (21½in)	19mm (¾in)	
Kneehole back panel	1	225mm (8⅞in)	520mm (20⅜in)	19mm (¾in)	
Other components:					
Plywood panel – back of pedestal	1	575mm (22¾in)	330mm (13⅛in)	6mm (¼in)	Ash plywood
Back top rail to pedestal	1	334mm (13¼in)	30mm (1¼in)	20mm (¾in)	Solid Ash
Tilt top stays	2	255mm (10in)	20mm (¾in)	10mm (⅜in)	Ash/Beech
Drawer front	1	500mm (19⅝in)	50mm (2in)	20mm (¾in)	Solid Ash
Drawer back	1	500mm (19⅝in)	35mm (1⅜in)	9mm (⅜in)	Beech
Drawer sides	2	380mm (15in)	50mm (2in)	9mm (⅜in)	Beech
Plywood bottom	1	490mm (19⅜in)	367mm (14½in)	6mm (¼in)	Birch plywood
Miscellaneous lippings					
All of same thickness varying from 12mm (½in) to 30mm (1⅛in) wide					Solid Ash
Pedestal shelves	2	546mm (21½in)	342mm (13½in)	19mm (¾in)	Chipboard (Lipped)
Pedestal base	1	565mm (22¼in)	342mm (13½in)	19mm (¾in)	Chipboard (Lipped)
Plinth	1	342mm (13½in)	58mm (2⅛in)	19mm (¾in)	Solid Ash

CHEST

This chest is made of pine, and relies on the
use of panelling to provide interest and break
up its surfaces. It is relatively simple to construct.

BASIC SKILLS

USING A COPING SAW	29
MARKING OUT	64
PLANING BOARDS FLAT	70
MOULDING EDGES	75
CUTTING AND FITTING MITRES	77
EDGE-JOINTING BOARDS	79
CUTTING AND FITTING MORTISE AND TENON JOINTS	80
GLUING UP	90
SANDING	96
BASIC FINISHING	100
STAINING	106

SPECIAL TECHNIQUES

HAUNCHING JOINTS	137
MAKING AND FITTING PANELS	139

Below: Underside of plinth showing glue blocks and plinth supports

Below right: The plinth and plywood base glued in place

HOW TO MAKE THE CHEST STEP-BY-STEP

1 The Carcase

The four corners of the carcase are formed by two front and two back uprights. Each front upright has a rebate on its inside edge and a stopped chamfer on its outside corner. The entire construction has five solid fielded panels, three at the front and one at each end. You should joint and plane these now, at the same time as making up the carcase.

The framework that holds these panels in place also makes up the main carcase. This is held together using stopped grooved frame mortise and tenon joints (see Special Technique, opposite). At the back, the top rail is much wider than on the rest of the construction, to accommodate the hinges. The back of the chest is grooved to hold 6mm (¼in) birch veneered plywood: this is readily available and looks similar to pine.

2 Fitting the Panels

Once you have made up the framework, to avoid putting a groove down a wrong edge, always mark the edges to be grooved in pencil. Work from the face side to ensure that the grooves line up with each other.

3 Making the Plinth

The plinth of the chest has four sides and in essence is the same construction as the pine bookcase (see the instructions on page 121). Cut out and mould the front of the plinth to improve the proportions and style of the piece. As with the bookcase, use both single and double ovolo mouldings to soften the look of the edges.

There is one important difference between this plinth and the bookcase, and this involves the fitting of a piece of plywood to the top of the plinth. This will eventually form the bottom of the chest. You will need to position the supporting blocks, which hold the plywood in place, slightly lower down, to produce, in effect, a 6mm (¼in) rebate into which you fit and glue the plywood. Any slight discrepancy between the plywood and the plinth will be concealed when you fit the main carcase later. Do this by screwing straight through the supporting blocks from below.

4 Making the Top

The top of the chest is made up of edge jointed boards. After planing it flat, bull-nose its front and ends using a smoothing plane or electric router. Cut out the back edge slightly to accommodate the decorative hinges and you may also need to round the bottom corner at the back a little to allow the lid to be lifted without it binding on the main carcase. Slotted bearers will help keep the top flat.

5 Double-Checking

Mould and check each panel for an accurate fit and dry clamp the chest, checking for any joints that may need adjusting. If the chest is to be stained and polished, to allow for movement later it is important to check that everything fits; sand and then stain and part-polish, before gluing up. If the wood is to be left natural, sand and just part-polish the panels before fitting.

6 Gluing Up

Glue the carcase first. Glue the two end panels, and leave to dry. Next, glue the front and back to the end panels. Make absolutely sure that any glue from the mortise and tenon joints that accidentally spills on the panels during gluing does not restrict the panels from moving due to moisture changes (see page 139). Next, glue the plinth together.

7 Fitting the Plinth

Fit the plinth by simply screwing from below through the supporting blocks. Ensure that the plinth protrudes a uniform distance from the carcase at the front and sides.

Left: The two front corner uprights have stopped chamfers as features and to prevent them being damaged

SPECIAL TECHNIQUES

HAUNCHING JOINTS

Tenons at the corners of rectangular frames often need to be 'inset' from the end so that the joint looks neat but has sufficient strength. This can be achieved by haunching the joint to give the tenon more width. Haunches are also used to fill in grooves that run from one end of a piece of wood to the other. It is common for the haunch to be as long as it is wide, although where it is used to fill in a groove, it is more important that it is the correct length. This is called a grooved frame mortise and tenon joint. On important ends, where the groove does not run all the way through and a haunch is preferable for strength, it is best to use a sloping haunch which will not be visible. Haunching a joint has the added benefit that, when cleaning up the mortise, there is less chance of damaging the shoulder when pulling back on the chisel. Joints cut with an electric router are often not haunched as the cutter can be stopped at the mortice.

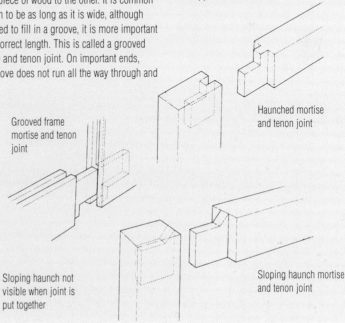

Grooved frame mortise and tenon joint

Haunched mortise and tenon joint

Sloping haunch not visible when joint is put together

Sloping haunch mortise and tenon joint

Right: Back of chest showing the wide top back rail holding the hinge in place

TIP

If you want to stain the chest an antique pine colour, do this first (before polishing), using a water-based stain which will accept any of the finishes described below. To avoid dark-coloured end grain, carefully seal it first with a thinned coat of polish before staining. Alternatively, you can dilute garnet French polish, apply using a brush and follow the instructions for sanding sealer (see page 103). If it dries patchily, it is still too thick. This will give you a quick and simple finish that colours and protects the wood simultaneously. Finish with clear/white paste wax.

REMEMBER TO ALWAYS NUMBER JOINTS

8 Fitting the Top

The top is simple to fit. Fasten the hinges in place before finishing to check that they are correctly positioned. Next, remove them, ensuring that you can see the holes clearly. Finish polishing the chest and then refit the hinges in their original position. This will guarantee that there is no chance of damaging the surface of the chest while fitting the hinges.

9 Finishing

The most suitable finishes for this chest are satin acrylic varnish (two to three coats finished with a light waxing of white/clear furniture paste wax to give a silky feel (see page 104); or, for a traditional polished finish, use sanding sealer or modified French polish or wax, buffing to a soft shine.

SPECIAL TECHNIQUES

MAKING AND FITTING RAISED AND FIELDED PANELS

First you need to produce the framework, marking out and cutting the mortise and tenon joints. This gives you the 'skeleton' of the carcase with 'holes' in the centre, which will be infilled with panels – grooves on the internal edges of this 'skeleton' will hold the panels in place.

Decide on the width of the groove needed to hold the panel. With this chest it is 6mm (¼in). If you use a plough plane to cut the grooves (see page 32), they will have to run from one end of the piece of wood to the other. If this is so, the mortise and tenons will need an extension on the shoulder of the tenon (haunching) to fill in the gap left by the groove (see page 137). Always work the grooves from the face side markings to guarantee that they all align.

Make sure you cut the panels wide enough and long enough to fit into the grooves, but do not make them so large that they strain the joints of the framework. You must also avoid making them too small, because if the panels later shrink, gaps will be created.

Generally, overall, the panel should be approximately 10–13mm (⅜–½in) wider and longer than the hole it is filling 5–6mm (³⁄₁₆–¼in) on either side), with the groove being 2mm (¹⁄₁₆in) deeper than the depth of the tongue on the panel. This produces a comfortable fit. When you are working in solid wood, it is easy to make mistakes. For example, a panel can often split because it has been fully glued in place. Avoid this by using only a dab of glue at the top and bottom centre of the panel to hold it at the centre of the framework. This will allow the wood to expand or contract from the middle.

A further, very noticeable, problem, concerns the positioning of the panels themselves. It is vital that they are fitted into the frame correctly. You can make a better job of this if you ensure the panel has a proper square tongue running all around its outside edge, allowing it to fit snugly into the groove. The tongue should preferably not be tapered because it will then sit in one position only. Sometimes (as on the moulding of the raised and fielded panels on this chest) you will have no choice: here, modern router cutters, designed specifically for sheet materials, have been used. In this case, careful fitting and the use of correctly dried wood are of paramount importance.

IMPORTANT

IMPORTANT

One mistake often to be seen on stained panels is where the panel shrinks, exposing white wood. When you are staining, it is best to stain and part polish the panel before assembly, so that when it moves, as it probably will, no light-coloured wood will become visible.

TYPES OF PANEL

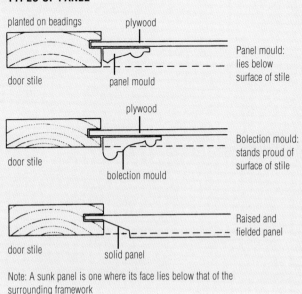

planted on beadings

plywood

door stile

panel mould

Panel mould: lies below surface of stile

plywood

door stile

bolection mould

Bolection mould: stands proud of surface of stile

door stile

solid panel

Raised and fielded panel

Note: A sunk panel is one where its face lies below that of the surrounding framework

MAKING A RAISED AND FIELDED PANEL BY HAND

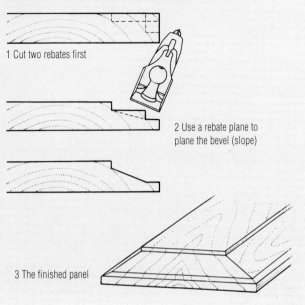

1 Cut two rebates first

2 Use a rebate plane to plane the bevel (slope)

3 The finished panel

WORKING DRAWINGS

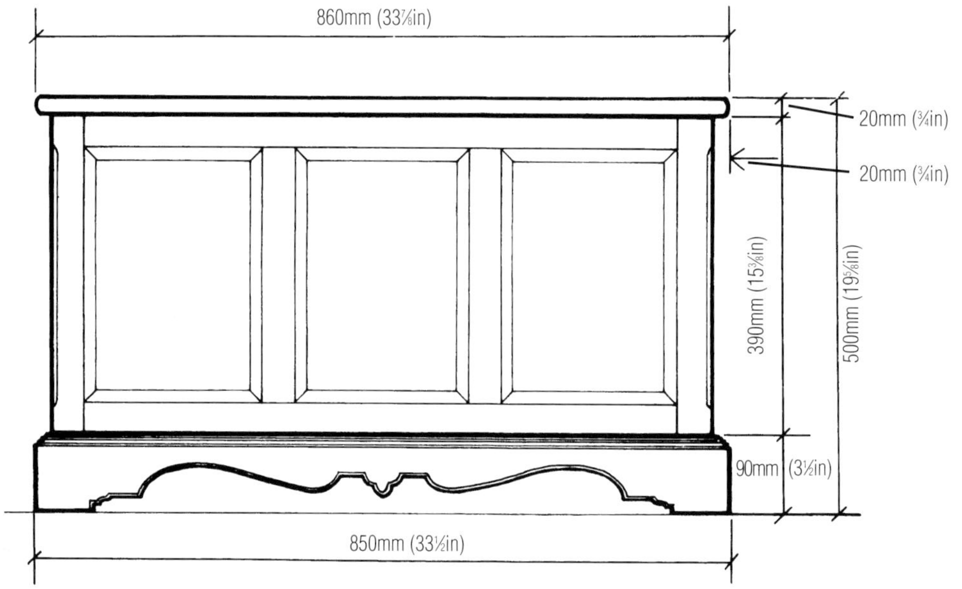

860mm (33⅞in)
20mm (¾in)
20mm (¾in)
390mm (15⅜in)
500mm (19⅝in)
90mm (3½in)
850mm (33½in)

FRONT ELEVATION

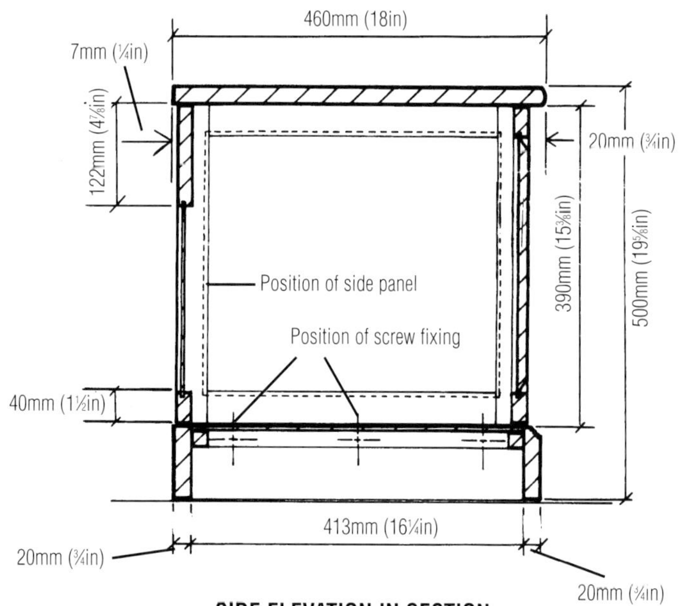

460mm (18in)
7mm (¼in)
122mm (4⅞in)
20mm (¾in)
390mm (15⅜in)
500mm (19⅝in)
Position of side panel
Position of screw fixing
40mm (1½in)
413mm (16¼in)
20mm (¾in)
20mm (¾in)

SIDE ELEVATION IN SECTION

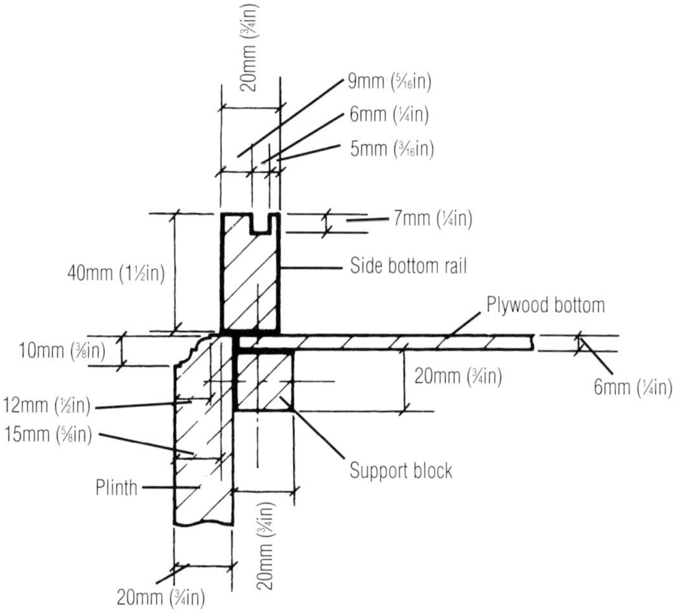

20mm (¾in)
9mm (5⁄16in)
6mm (¼in)
5mm (3⁄16in)
7mm (¼in)
40mm (1½in)
Side bottom rail
Plywood bottom
10mm (⅜in)
20mm (¾in)
6mm (¼in)
12mm (½in)
15mm (⅝in)
Support block
Plinth
20mm (¾in)
20mm (¾in)

DETAIL OF SECTION THROUGH PLINTH

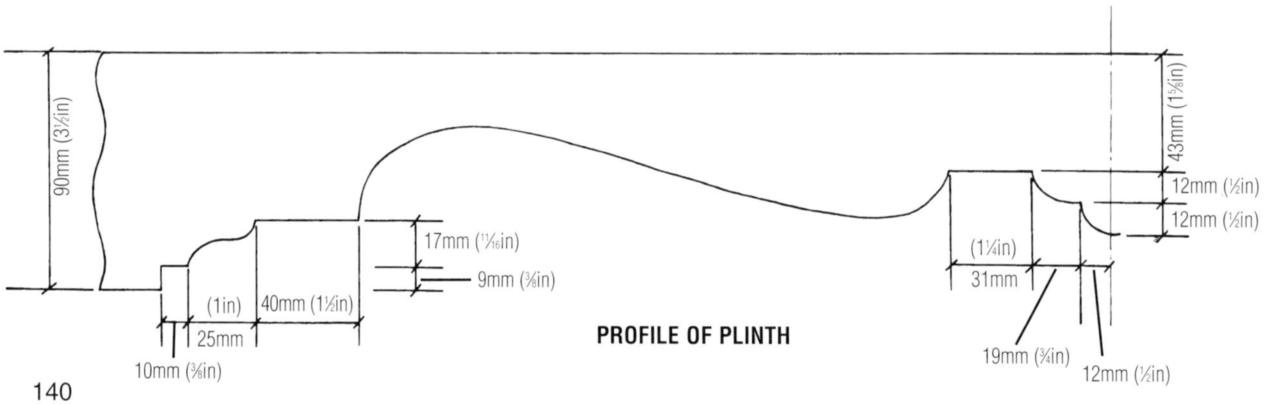

90mm (3½in)
43mm (1⅝in)
12mm (½in)
12mm (½in)
17mm (11⁄16in)
9mm (⅜in)
(1in)
40mm (1½in)
25mm
10mm (⅜in)
(1¼in)
31mm
19mm (¾in)
12mm (½in)

PROFILE OF PLINTH

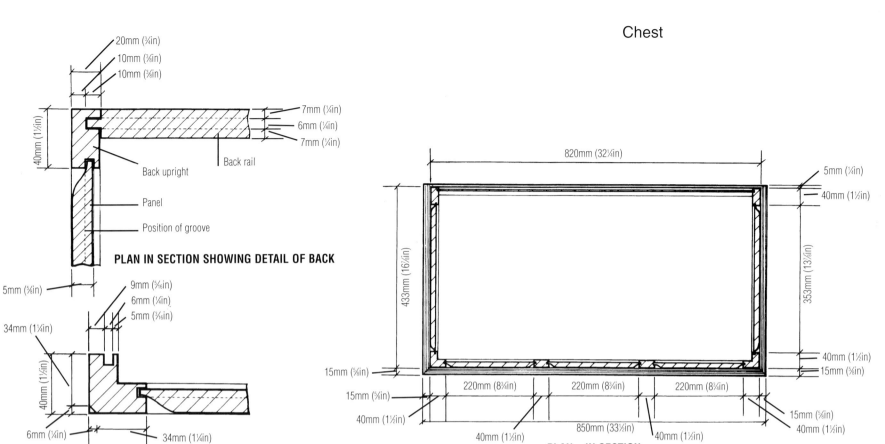

PLAN IN SECTION SHOWING DETAIL OF BACK

DETAIL OF FRONT CORNER UPRIGHT

PLAN – IN SECTION

CUTTING LIST

COMPONENT	NUMBER	LENGTH	WIDTH	THICKNESS	COMMENTS
Top	1	860mm (33⅞in)	460mm (18in)	20mm (¾in)	Made up of 3 pieces edge jointed together
Front uprights	2	390mm (15⅜in)	40mm (1½in)	40mm (1½in)	
Back uprights	2	390mm (15⅜in)	40mm (1½in)	20mm (¾in)	
Side rails top and bottom	4	391mm (15⅜in)	40mm (1½in)	20mm (¾in)	Includes tenons
Front rails top and bottom	2	782mm (30¾in)	40mm (1½in)	20mm (¾in)	Includes tenons
Central muntin	2	350mm (13⅜in)	40mm (1½in)	20mm (¾in)	Includes tenons
Top back rail	1	800mm (31½in)	122mm (4⅞in)	20mm (¾in)	Includes tenons
Bottom back rail	1	800mm (31½in)	40mm (1½in)	20mm (¾in)	Includes tenons
Plywood back	1	240mm (9½in)	792mm (31¼in)	6mm (¼in)	Birch plywood
Plinth – front	1	850mm (33½in)	90mm (3½in)	20mm (¾in)	
Plinth – sides	2	453mm (17¾in)	90mm (3½in)	20mm (¾in)	
Plinth – back	1	810mm (32in)	90mm (3½in)	20mm (¾in)	
Plywood base	1	413mm (16¼in)	820mm (32¼in)	6mm (¼in)	Birch plywood
Plinth supports	2	810mm (32in)	20mm (¾in)	20mm (¾in)	
Plinth supports	4	373mm (14¾in)	20mm (¾in)	20mm (¾in)	
Glue blocks			20mm (¾in)	20mm (¾in)	Out of scrap
Front panels	3	320mm (12⅞in)	232mm (9¼in)	15mm (⅝in)	Jointed up in 2 pieces
Side panels	2	320mm (12⅞in)	365mm (14⅜in)	15mm (⅝in)	Jointed up in 2 pieces

141

BEDSIDE CABINET

This simple cabinet has solid sides, shelf, base and top, all of which involve the techniques of planing boards flat and cutting wide housing joints. This project will also teach you how to fit a door.

BASIC SKILLS

USING A COPING SAW	29
MARKING OUT	64
PLANING BOARDS FLAT	70
EDGE-JOINTING BOARDS	79
CUTTING AND FITTING MORTISE AND TENON JOINTS	80
CUTTING AND FITTING HOUSING JOINTS	84
GLUING UP	90
SANDING	96
BASIC FINISHING	100
HAUNCHING JOINTS	137
MAKING A RAISED AND FIELDED PANEL	139
FITTING A DOOR PANEL	149

SPECIAL TECHNIQUES

MARKING OUT TWIN STUB TENONS	144
MAKING AND FITTING DOORS	146

HOW TO MAKE THE CABINET STEP-BY-STEP

1 Making the Carcase
First, cut and plane the wood to size, and joint up the sides, shelf and base (as well as the top). Plane flat and cut them to size. The shelf and base are fastened into place using stopped barefaced housing joints. Next, mark out and cut the back and front top rail. Secure to the sides using twin stub tenons (see opposite).

Groove the back of the cabinet to hold the 6mm (¼in) plywood back. The shelf sits in front of the plywood back and is therefore not grooved.

2 Making the Plinth
Construct the plinth of this bedside cabinet in the same way as the bookcase plinth (see page 121), except that since this one is wider, it is a good idea to put slots in the supporting blocks to allow for possible expansion and contraction of the carcase.

3 Making the Top
Make the top by edge jointing two pieces of wood and after planing flat, trim it to size. Mark the rounds of the two front corners using a tin lid as a template and cut using a coping saw. Smooth them by sanding.

4 The Decoration
The Ovolo mouldings on the two ends and front of the top (both top and bottom) match the plinth. Use a quirk bead (see page 123) to decorate the outside front edge of both sides and along the top edge of the shelf to soften the edges gently.

5 Making the Door
The next stage is to make the door (see Special Technique page 146). The corner joints of the frame are moulded groove frame mortise and tenons (see page 80). Mark and cut these joints – they will need to be haunched if you cut the grooves using a combination plane (see page 137). For more details on making and fitting the panel, see page 139.

6 Sanding and Gluing
After making the carcase, plinth, top and door, sand all internal faces. Seal them if you wish, to avoid damage by

144

SPECIAL TECHNIQUES

MARKING OUT TWIN STUB TENONS

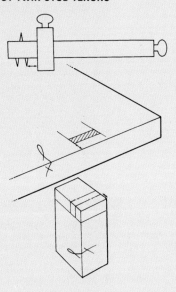

Set up a marking gauge to mark on the position of the first tenon on one half of the joint; mark out the mortise on the same setting. Mark out the first part of all stub tenon joints from this same setting.

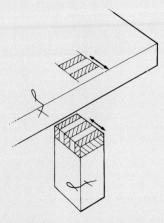

Then alter the mortise gauge to mark out the second mortise and tenon. Always work from face side/edge marks

glue spillage. Next glue the carcase and plinth and fit together.

7 Fitting the Top
Hold the top in place by screwing through the top front rail, using stretcher plates at the back to allow the wood to move if it needs to (see page 121).

8 Finishing
You can create a natural-looking finish by using sanding sealer and paste wax, although you may find that this will mark if the furniture is not looked after carefully. If you require extra protection, use a satin acrylic or oil-based varnish instead (see page 104).

Below: As the plywood back panel is small, it has been grooved into position. On chests of drawers or large cabinets, it is best to use rebates and screw through fillets from the back. This will allow access should the drawer swell and be held fast in place

SPECIAL TECHNIQUES

When fitting hinges, always fit only one screw at a time, checking that the door still opens and closes in the correct place after each one.

When fitting the door to the carcase, mark on the exact position with a knife to the top or bottom of each hinge only. Mark on the other side (i.e. the length) of the hinge by using the hinge itself as a template, again not forgetting to allow for the creep of the chisel. Use the previously set-up gauges to mark on the width and depth of the hinges and chop out carefully.

The final fit of a door is important, as unsightly gaps or twisted door frames, causing the door to stand proud, are easily seen defects. If you practise and steadily improve the accuracy of your marking out, these will not be frustrating problems. After polishing, fit door stops and handles as required.

Where two doors meet (looking down) they can butt together or have their edges rebated to fit each other

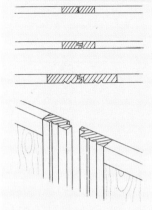

MAKING AND FITTING DOORS

There are several ways to fit doors: this is one simple method that works.

A door is a piece of movable joinery which should fit accurately into its opening. If a door is hung incorrectly, it will either scrape against the sides or bottom, appear lop-sided, or have uneven gaps around its edges.

MAKING THE DOOR

The door itself (when made to a traditional construction rather than merely being cut from man-made sheet materials), consists of a framework of four lengths of wood, mortised and tenoned into each other. The centre is infilled with a solid panel held in grooves. Properly constructed, this sort of framework will keep the door flat and true and allow the panel to expand or contract if it needs to. See page 139 for making the panel.

I have used moulded grooved mortise and tenon joints (see pages 80, 139 and 149) on the door of this bedside cabinet, which will accommodate the decorative ovolo moulding by being neatly mitred at the corners.

INITIAL FITTING OF THE DOOR

When you have made and assembled the door, true up its bottom edge with a smoothing plane to make it stand perfectly upright. Next make the door fit the carcase on the hinge side by careful planing to make it match the cabinet. Then fit the top and other side of the door, leaving a gap of around 0.75mm (¹⁄₃₂in) between the carcase and the door. If you feel it helps, you can very slightly bevel the edges of the door towards the back which will assist in the final fitting.

THE HINGES

Brass butt hinges are the most common type used on traditional doors. They are usually fitted equally into both the door opening and the stile of the door. You may however prefer to fit them into the door only, which is a little easier as you will only have to cut out recesses on the door stile to hold the hinges.

WHERE TO PUT HINGES

There is no fixed rule for the position of hinges. The best rule in fact is the rule of thumb – literally. Put the door on a bench (with the stile parallel to the front of the bench) and put a thumb from each hand an equal distance from the top and bottom edges of the door. If this is obviously too far apart, slowly bring your thumbs together, moving equally until you think you are in the right area. It is simply a matter of judgement, but is generally just less than a quarter of the length of the stile measured from the top or bottom edge of the door. Look at other pieces of furniture around the house if you need guidance.

HANGING THE DOOR

Fit the hinges to the door first. Put the door frame in a vice and lightly mark the position of the bottom edge of each hinge with a sharp knife,

using a square to continue this knife line across the edge of the door stile. Next put the hinge on the door stile so that it just covers this first knife line and lightly mark the position of the top of the hinge with the knife. This small movement of the hinge allows for the creep of the chisel when chopping out the recess. Put two light pencil lines down the front of the stile to show where to stop and start the marking gauge when marking on the depth of the hinge.

As well as the length, you must also allow for chisel creep on the width and depth of the hinge. To do this set up a marking gauge to a measurement of about 0.25mm (¹⁄₆₄in) less than half the total width of the hinge. Next, set up a second gauge to around 0.25mm (¹⁄₆₄in) less than half of the total thickness of the hinge. Or, more simply, set up each measurement and then reduce it by a tiny fraction!

The best way to establish half the width is to pick up the hinge, open it up fully and measure it accurately. Let's say this equals 28mm (1¹⁄₈in). Half of this is 14mm (⁹⁄₁₆in), so set the marking gauge to this measurement, less the amount to be allowed for creep.

You can now use both marking gauges to mark the positions of the width and the depth of the hinge. Finally, chop out the hinge recess by carefully working back to the gauge lines with a chisel.

Note if you have only one marking gauge, mark the width first, reset and then mark the depth.

Allowing for 'creep' when chopping out hinge recesses: move the hinge just over the first knife line before marking on the position of the other end of the hinge

Left: Select good quality fittings for doors and drawers to add the finishing touch

1 Ring handle
2 Drop handles
3 Cabinet handle
4 Domed knob
5 Flat knob
6 Plate handle
7 Butt hinge
8 Fretted plate handle
9 Snake hinge
10 H hinge
11 Magnetic catch
12 Ball catch
13 Double ball catch

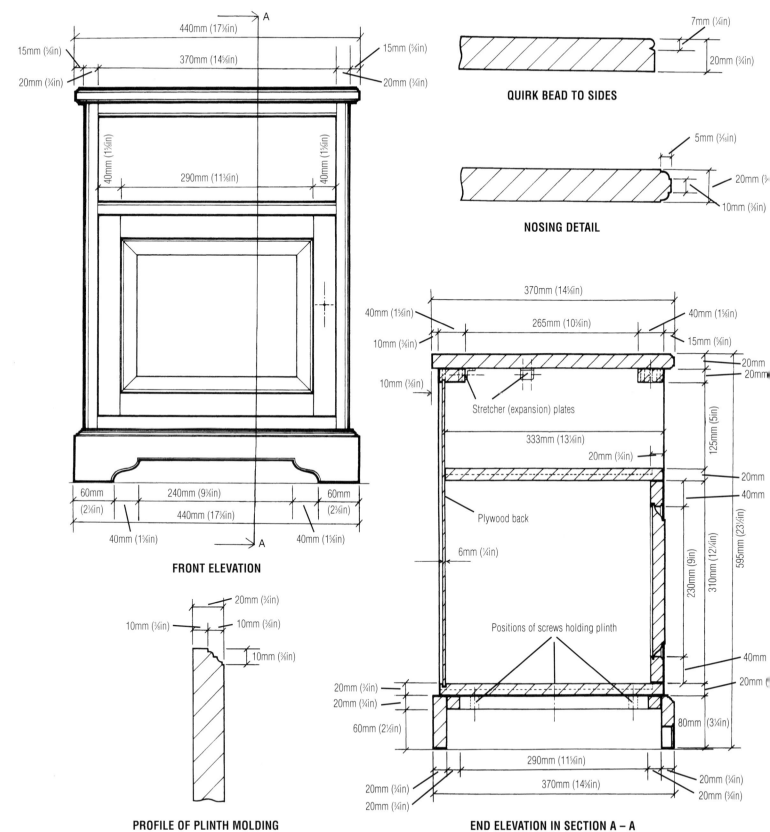

440mm (17⅜in)

370mm (14⅝in)

15mm (⅝in)

15mm (⅝in)

20mm (¾in)

20mm (¾in)

40mm (1⅝in)

40mm (1⅝in)

290mm (11⅜in)

40mm (1⅝in)

60mm (2⅜in)

240mm (9⅜in)

60mm (2⅜in)

440mm (17⅜in)

40mm (1⅝in)

40mm (1⅝in)

FRONT ELEVATION

7mm (¼in)

20mm (¾in)

QUIRK BEAD TO SIDES

5mm (³⁄₁₆in)

20mm (¾in)

10mm (⅜in)

NOSING DETAIL

370mm (14⅝in)

265mm (10⅜in)

40mm (1⅝in)

40mm (1⅝in)

10mm (⅜in)

15mm (⅝in)

20mm

20mm

10mm (⅜in)

Stretcher (expansion) plates

125mm (5in)

333mm (13⅛in)

20mm (¾in)

20mm

Plywood back

40mm

230mm (9in)

310mm (12¼in)

595mm (23⅜in)

6mm (¼in)

Positions of screws holding plinth

40mm

20mm (¾in)

20mm (¾in)

60mm (2½in)

80mm (3¼in)

290mm (11⅝in)

20mm (¾in)

370mm (14⅝in)

20mm (¾in)

20mm (¾in)

20mm (¾in)

END ELEVATION IN SECTION A – A

20mm (¾in)

10mm (⅜in)

10mm (⅜in)

10mm (⅜in)

PROFILE OF PLINTH MOLDING

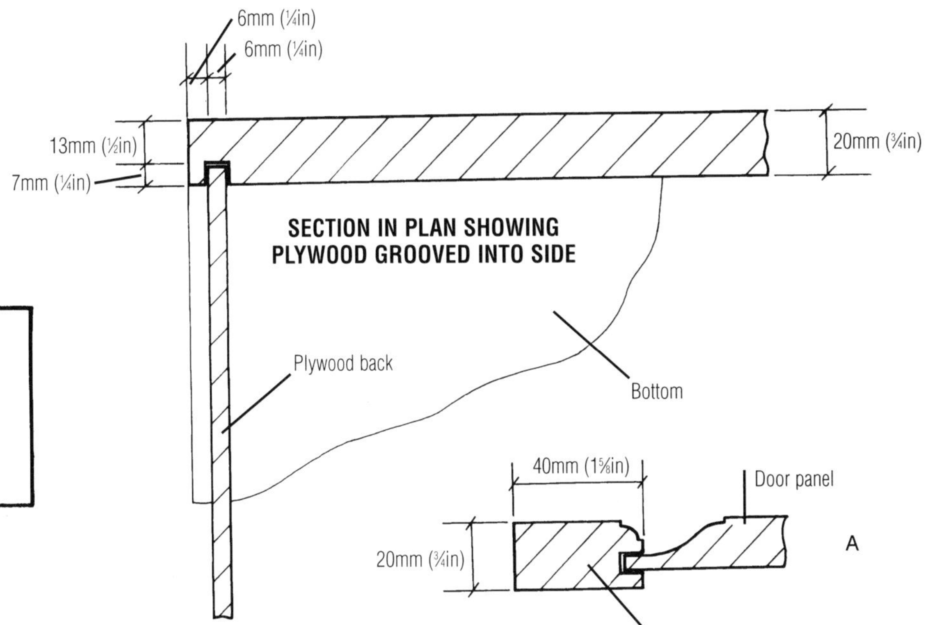

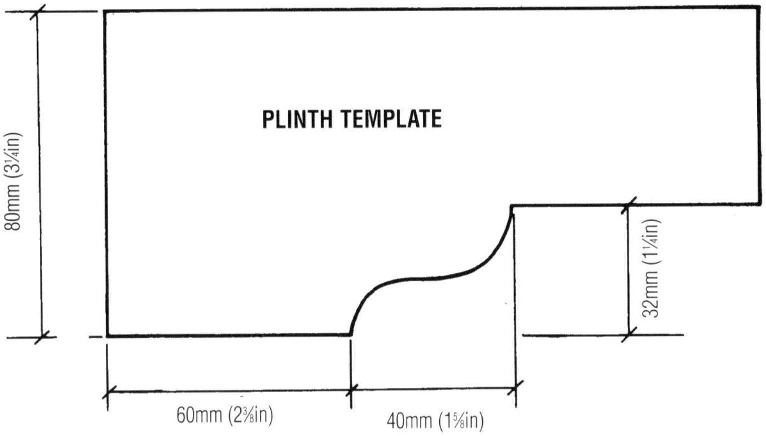

As this is a small door, the panel can either be fitted into grooves (illustration A) or put into a moulded frame which has a rebate. The fillet is pinned into position and, in order to hold the panel, the stile should be slightly thicker (illustration B).

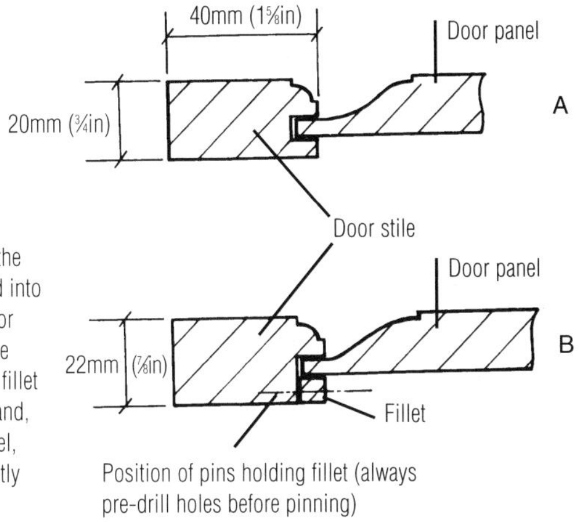

CUTTING LIST

COMPONENT	NUMBER	LENGTH	WIDTH	THICKNESS	COMMENTS
Top	1	440mm (17⅜in)	370mm (14⅝in)	20mm (¾in)	Made up of 3 pieces edge jointed together
Shelf	1	390mm (15⅝in)	333mm (13⅛in)	20mm (¾in)	Includes housings. Jointed up in 3 pieces
Bottom	1	390mm (15⅝in)	345mm (13⅝in)	20mm (¾in)	Made up of 3 pieces edge jointed together. Includes housings jointed up in 3 pieces
Sides	2	495mm (19½in)	345mm (13⅝in)	20mm (¾in)	
Front and back top rails	2	390mm (15⅝in)	40mm (1⅝in)	20mm (¾in)	Includes tenons
Plinth – front	1	440mm (17⅜in)	80mm (3¼in)	20mm (¾in)	
Plinth – sides	2	370mm (14⅝in)	80mm (3¼in)	20mm (¾in)	
Plinth – back	1	400mm (15⅞in)	80mm (3¼in)	20mm (¾in)	
Glue blocks			20mm (¾in)	20mm (¾in)	Out of scrap
Door stiles	2	310mm (12¼in)	40mm (1⅝in)	20mm (¾in)	See working drawings reference grooves or rebates
Door rails	2	330mm (12⅞in)	40mm (1⅝in)	20mm (¾in)	Includes tenons
Door panel	1	242mm (9½in)	302mm (11⅞in)	15mm (⅝in)	Jointed up in 2 pieces
Plywood back	1	467mm (18½in)	382mm (15⅛in)	6mm (¼in)	Birch plywood

SMALL TABLE WITH DRAWER

This small oak table is straightforward except for the one extra that makes it a little more complicated – namely the drawer. Fitting drawers can separate the amateur from the professional, yet if you follow a basic procedure, with practice you will find that the job is actually quite simple.

BASIC SKILLS

MARKING OUT	64
PLANING BOARDS FLAT	70
MOULDING EDGES	75
EDGE-JOINTING BOARDS	79
CUTTING AND FITTING MORTISE AND TENON JOINTS	80
MARKING OUT AND CUTTING DOVETAILS	85
GLUING UP	90
BASIC STAINING AND POLISHING OF HARDWOODS	100
FITTING A TOP	121
FITTING A DUST PANEL (GROOVING)	129
MARKING OUT TWIN STUB MORTISE AND TENON JOINTS	144

SPECIAL TECHNIQUES

MAKING AND FITTING DRAWERS	154

If you turn the legs yourself it is a good idea to turn them before cutting the mortises out for the rails: otherwise, the fact that some wood has been removed will increase the chance of the leg vibrating on the lathe as it spins due to centrifugal force.

Below: Twin stub tenons. the tenons can be made narrower, creating edge shoulders, as this prevents the mortise being damaged during cutting

HOW TO MAKE THE TABLE STEP-BY-STEP

1 Preparing the Carcase

Start by cutting and preparing the wood for the carcase: make two front rails, one wide back rail and two wide side rails, as well as four legs and four lengths for the stretchers (bottom rails).

2 Making the Legs

The legs on this table are turned on a lathe. Turning is a skill in itself and is not covered in this book: the further reading on page 158 will help. If you do not want to turn the legs yourself you can buy ready-turned legs or substitute the legs for square ones – extra decorations, such as stopped chamfers on the corners or flutes, will help to keep the table in proportion.

Whatever type of leg you choose, mark on in pencil the approximate positions of the mortise and tenon joints so that you don't make a mistake.

3 Marking the Carcase

The joints making up the carcase are simple stopped mortise and tenons (see page 80). As usual, when marking these out, always work from the face side and edge marks – but in this case you will need to reset the stock of your mortise gauge after marking out the tenons to allow for the rails to sit back from the front edge of the legs.

The two sets of twin stub tenons on the top front rails are cut out in the same way as normal tenons, but cut out the waste in the centre with a coping saw and clean up with a bevel-edged chisel. This is the same technique used for cutting out waste between the pins on dovetail joints. After making up the carcase and checking that the joints fit, prepare the top by edge-jointing two pieces together (see page 79). Leave to dry and trim to size.

4 Making and Fitting the Drawer Carcase

This piece of furniture has a traditional drawer supported and steered by runners, kickers and guides – see Special Technique (page 154) for how to mark out, cut, glue, fit and clean up drawers.

5 Making the Decorative Edges

Lightly round the square corners of the legs except those that meet the two top front rails. Round the four edges of the bottom rails too, but a little more than on the legs. Work an ovolo mould around the ends and front edge of the top, as well as the bottom outside edge of the back and side rails (see page 123).

6 Fitting a Dust Panel

You can add an additional touch of quality to furniture by fitting a dust panel. This is simply a plywood panel grooved into the carcase below a drawer. In this case, the plywood fits into the back edge of the bottom front rail and the inside edge of the runners and back rail. A dust panel neatly finishes off the underside of a carcase, and in furniture with multiple drawers, stops objects falling from one drawer·into the one below it. Next, glue the carcase together ready for fitting the top.

7 Cleaning and Sanding

Now clean up the entire work, including the top ends of the legs where the rails are fitted into them. This will guarantee the top sits flush. Next, sand ready for finishing. You can sand, stain and part-polish before

Left: Dry clamping showing runners, kickers and guides. On large constructions, the top rails can be dovetailed into the sides and blocked out for rigidity. Runners and kickers can then be held in grooves or screwed and glued into place afterwards for ease of fitting

gluing if you prefer, or carry out the staining and polishing process later on the fully glued-up project.

8 Fitting the Top

You will require a cranked or stubby screwdriver. Secure the top using wood screws fastened through the top rail. Use stretcher plates, or buttons (see page 121), at the back to allow the top to move due to changes in moisture content.

9 Staining

Oak may be stained dark to resemble old oak furniture, or you could keep it natural if you prefer. A water-based stain will give the best depth of colour and for best results apply the stain with a brush, wiping it off again with a cloth, and never allowing the stain to dry out. Do not forget to raise the grain first (see page 107). A dash of ammonia will help the stain to bite into the wood.

10 Finishing

For the simplest and most effective finish apply three to four coats of modified or transparent French polish, which dries clear. You could use thinned garnet or button French polish to tone the work if you prefer. Follow this by waxing the furniture with a soft paste wax to pull out a top quality natural sheen (see page 101).

153

SPECIAL TECHNIQUES

MAKING AND FITTING DRAWERS

Drawers are effectively deep trays, sliding in and out of a carcase. This means that to fit one you will have to consider both the drawer and the parts it slides on.

POINTS TO CONSIDER WHEN MAKING THE CARCASE

When making up the carcase, ensure that it is as square as possible. On traditional drawers there are three sets of rails which guide the drawer into place. These are the runners (which the drawer sits on), the kickers, which look similar to the runners except that they run along the top of the drawer sides (preventing the drawer from toppling forward as it is pulled outwards), and the guides, which steer the drawer in the carcase. On multiple sets of drawers, say a three-drawer chest, you can make the kicker of one drawer become the runner for the drawer above it.

Joint the runners and kickers either into the front and back rails of the carcase or screw and glue to the sides for strength and support. The guides are screwed and glued into place. Even though all three perform totally separate tasks each must run parallel and at the same time be at 90 degrees to the front of the carcase. If not, the drawer will either bind, fit sloppily or even worse, will not open and close properly. If you find that the carcase is a little out of square, still try to make the kickers, guides and runners run as true and accurately as you can.

MAKING THE DRAWER

A drawer is made up of two sides, a front, a back and a bottom. The fronts of most drawers are usually made from a decorative wood, most often the same as the rest of the cabinet. This is usually a little thicker than the sides and back.

Before making the drawer, plane the left and right drawer sides and make them fit exactly their position in the drawer space. Check they slide in and

out properly. If you select wood with the grain running towards the back of the drawer you can lightly clean up the sides later in final fitting without damaging the front.

You can either make the length of the back fit the opening exactly, or leave it a little longer on its length to allow for cleaning up (see page 95). If you cut the back exactly to size you must mark out the joints extremely accurately as there will be only a small amount of wood for cleaning up later. Fit the front to width but let the length of the front overhang very slightly. If you really want to be professional, make the ends of the drawer front bevel very slightly inwards so that the drawer front actually fits into the carcase a little before becoming, in effect, wedged in place. Work as accurately as you can. With this method you can carefully take off one or two shavings at a time with a smoothing plane after assembly, as you fit the drawer. Next groove the drawer sides and front (make sure you put the groove where it will be covered by the dovetails, see below). Once you know the position of the groove, you can cut and plane the back of the drawer to its correct width.

MAKING THE DOVETAIL JOINTS

Mark out and cut the dovetail joints (see page 85) ensuring that the waste is cleaned out from the bottom of each joint. Use lapped dovetails for the joints at the front of the drawer, but straightforward through dovetails for the two at the back. Always work with the face side and face edge marks in uniform positions – i.e. face side marks pointing inside the drawer and face edge marks facing the bottom.

GLUING THE DRAWER

Make sure that you have cleaned up, sanded and sealed (if you wish) all internal faces before gluing the drawer together. It is very important that when you glue up the drawer, it lies totally flat and is not in any form of twist. When the glue has dried, carefully clean up the dovetails and check the fit of the drawer by first offering the back of the drawer up to the carcase. On deep drawers, you can put drawer supports underneath to provide extra

HOW A DRAWER IS SUPPORTED IN A CARCASE

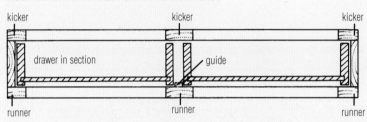

kicker · kicker · kicker

drawer in section · guide

runner · runner · runner

Remember to put the groove where it will be hidden by the dovetails

strength for the bottom. After fitting these, slide the drawer bottom into place. Use birch plywood or better still, for a totally traditional drawer, solid cedar of Lebanon for the bottom. Do not forget that solid wood needs to be able to expand and contract, so do not glue it in place, but screw from underneath into the back of the drawer through slotted holes.

FITTING THE DRAWER

Fit the drawer after cleaning up the dovetails with a smoothing plane (see page 95) and then take off a shaving at a time as needed, checking and rechecking where necessary. If you wax the runners, kickers and guides of the carcase before fitting, marks will appear on the drawer showing which areas should be planed off first. After fitting the drawer, lightly sand and wax it (using beeswax or paraffin wax) to help it run smoothly. Drawer stops (not shown on the working drawing) are fitted to the front rail of the cabinet underneath the drawer bottom.

DIFFERENT TYPES OF DRAWER

If you wish to create a more decorative drawer, you can adapt it slightly by fitting a cock beading around the drawer front (see below). This will make it a little easier to plane and fit into the carcase. Another method is to make a drawer that has a false front, screwing it in place from behind. This will stand proud of the carcase and hide any slight gaps between the drawer and drawer space. In either case it is important to achieve a good fit, as the drawer body will either wobble or bind in places if you do not.

You do not necessarily have to make up a drawer using dovetail joints and you may prefer instead to use finger joints or lapped joints which are much easier to make. But for pure strength and decorative effect, a good, well-proportioned dovetail joint wins every time.

Chamfering the back top edge of the drawer sides prevents air being trapped when the drawer is closed. It also makes it easier to slide the drawer in and out

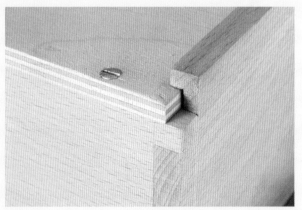

Underside of drawer: the drawer bottom slides into a groove from the back

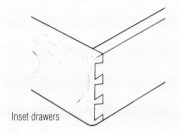

Inset drawers

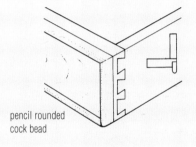

pencil rounded cock bead

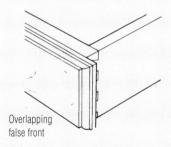

Overlapping false front

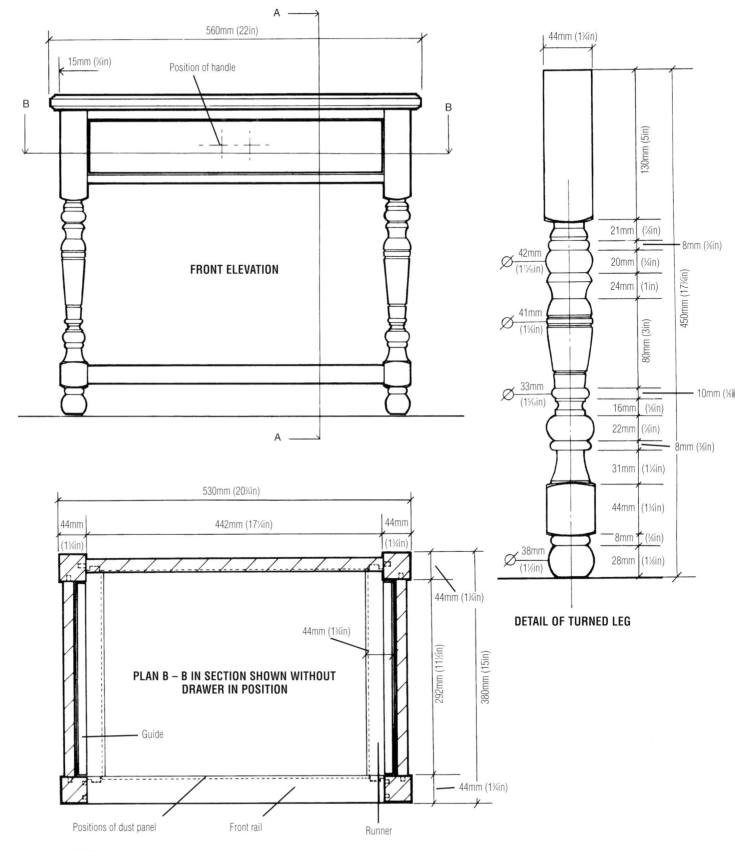

A

560mm (22in)

15mm (⅝in)

Position of handle

B   B

FRONT ELEVATION

A

530mm (20⅞in)

44mm (1¾in)   442mm (17¼in)   44mm (1¾in)

44mm (1¾in)

44mm (1¾in)

PLAN B – B IN SECTION SHOWN WITHOUT DRAWER IN POSITION

292mm (11½in)   380mm (15in)

Guide

44mm (1¾in)

Positions of dust panel   Front rail   Runner

44mm (1¾in)

130mm (5in)

21mm (⅞in)   8mm (⅜in)

42mm (1¹¹⁄₁₆in)

20mm (¾in)

24mm (1in)

41mm (1⅝in)

450mm (17¾in)

80mm (3in)

33mm (1⁵⁄₁₆in)   10mm (⅜

16mm (⅝in)

22mm (⅞in)   8mm (⅜in)

31mm (1¼in)

44mm (1¾in)

8mm (⅜in)

38mm (1½in)   28mm (1⅛in)

DETAIL OF TURNED LEG

156

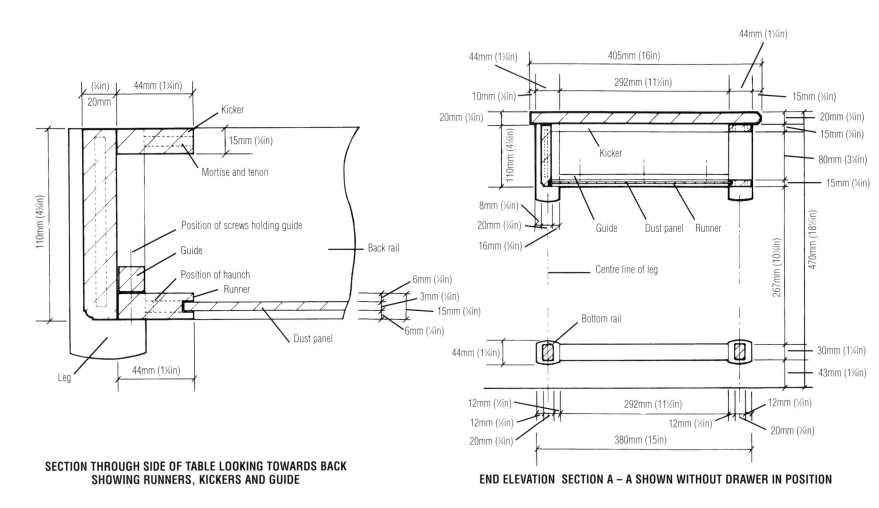

**SECTION THROUGH SIDE OF TABLE LOOKING TOWARDS BACK
SHOWING RUNNERS, KICKERS AND GUIDE**

END ELEVATION SECTION A – A SHOWN WITHOUT DRAWER IN POSITION

CUTTING LIST

COMPONENT	NUMBER	LENGTH	WIDTH	THICKNESS	COMMENTS
Top	1	560mm (22in)	405mm (16in)	20mm (¾in)	Jointed up in 2 pieces
Legs	4	450mm (17¾in)	44mm (1¾in)	44mm (1¾in)	
Bottom rails	2	480mm (18¾in)	30mm (1¼in)	20mm (¾in)	Includes tenons
Bottom rails	2	330mm (13in)	30mm (1¼in)	20mm (¾in)	Includes tenons
Top side rails	2	330mm (13in)	110mm (4⅜in)	20mm (¾in)	Includes tenons
Top back rail	1	480mm (18¾in)	110mm (4⅜in)	20mm (¾in)	Includes tenons
Top front rails	2	464mm (18¼in)	44mm (1¾in)	15mm (⅝in)	Includes tenons
Runners	2	330mm (13in)	44mm (1¾in)	15mm (⅝in)	Includes tenons
Kickers	2	330mm (13in)	44mm (1¾in)	15mm (⅝in)	Includes tenons
Guides	2	292mm (11½in)	16mm (⅝in)	16mm (⅝in)	
Dust panel	1	398mm (15½in)	320mm (12⅝in)	3mm (⅛in)	Birch plywood
Drawer front	1	442mm (17¼in)	80mm (3⅛in)	20mm (¾in)	
Drawer sides	2	288mm (11⅜in)	80mm (3⅛in)	9mm (⅜in)	Beech
Drawer back	1	442mm (17¼in)	62mm (2⅜in)	9mm (⅜in)	Beech
Drawer bottom	1	432mm (17in)	284mm (11¼in)	6mm (¼in)	Birch plywood

USEFUL ADDRESSES

FINNEY'S WOOD FINISHES
66–68 Thirlwell Road
Sheffield S8 9TF
UK
Telephone: 0114 258 8399
Email: info@mdfinney.co.uk
www.mdfinney.co.uk

STANLEY TOOLS INTERNATIONAL

UK
The Stanley Works Limited
Stanley Tools Division
Europa View
Sheffield Business Park
Sheffield S9 1XH
UK
Telephone: 0114 244 8883
Fax: 0114 273 9038
www.stanleyworks.com

USA
Stanley Tools Ltd
600 Myrtle Street
New Britain CT 06050
USA
Telephone: (203) 225 5111
Fax: (203) 827 5829

ASIA PACIFIC
Stanley Works Asia Pacific Ltd
Singapore
25 Senoko South
Woodland East Industrial Estate
Singapore 2775
Telephone: (65) 752 2001
Fax: (65) 752 2697
752 2018

AUSTRALIA
The Stanley Works Pty, Ltd
PO Box 62
58 Dougharty Road
Heidelberg West 3081
Victoria
Australia
Telephone: (61) (3) 459 1144
Fax: (61) (3) 458 2865

The Stanley Works Pty, Ltd
PO Box 21
95 Albert Road
Moonah 7009
Tasmania

Australia
Telephone: (61) (02) 280 295
Fax: (61) (02) 284 662

NEW ZEALAND
Stanley Tools (NZ) Ltd
PO Box 12–582
Penrose
Auckland
New Zealand
Telephone: (64) (9) 642 102
Fax: (64) (9) 666 302

INDONESIA
PT Stanley Works Ind.
II/55–57 Rungkut Industri Street
Surabaya
Indonesia

AUSTRIA
Egide Walschaertraat 14–16
2800 Mechelen
Belgium
Telephone: 00 3215 473780
Fax: 00 3215 473782

BELGIUM
Stanley Works Belgium NV
Brouwenjstraat
9880 Aalter
Belgium
Telephone: (32) (91) 746933
Fax: (32) (91) 746243

DENMARK AND ICELAND
Stanley vaerktoej ApS
Hoeje Tastrup Vej 30
Dk–2630 Tastrup
Denmark
Telephone: (45) (43) 71 33 34
Fax: (45) (43) 71 33 88

FINLAND
Suomen Stanley Oy
PO Box 71
SF–00381 Helsinki, 38
Finland
Telephone: Helsinki (358) (0) 558551
Fax: (358) (0) 558551

FRANCE
Stanley – Mabo SA
Boite Postale 1579
25009 Besançon Cedex
France
Telephone: (33) (81) 663636

Fax: (33) (81) 882171

GERMANY
Stanley Germany, Inc.
Zweigniederiassung, Essen
P.O. Box 16 44 09
Butzgenweg 2 0–4300 Essen–16
Germany
Telephone: (49) (201) 408053
Fax: (49) (201) 409222

GREECE
The Stanley Works Ltd
PO Box 75018, 17610 Kallithea
Athens
Greece
Telephone: (30) (1) 9225541
Fax: (30) (1) 9215930

ITALY
Stanley tools SPA
Via Trieste 1
22060 Figino Serenza (CO)
Italy
Telephone: (39) (31) 780359
Fax: (39) (31) 781094

LUXEMBOURG
Contact Stanley office in Netherlands

NETHERLANDS
Stanley Works (Nederland) BV
Sand-Ambachtstraat 95
"s-Gravenzande
Netherlands
Telephone: (31) 1748 12001
Fax: (31) 1748 13861

SPAIN
Contact Stanley office in Besançon,
France

SWEDEN
Stanley Svenska AB
Box 1054
Datavagen 31
S 436 00 Askim
Sweden
Telephone: (46) (31) 289770
Fax: (46) (31) 288099

SWITZERLAND
Contact Stanley office in "s-
Gravenzande, Netherlands

FURTHER READING

George Buchanan, *The Illustrated Handbook of Furniture Restoration*, B.T. Batsford, London, 1985

Thomas Corkhill, *A Glossary of Wood*, Stobart and Son Ltd, London, 1988

H.E. Desch, *Timber: Its Structure, Properties and Utilisation*, Macmillan, London, 1985

Franklin Gottshall, *How to Design and Construct Period Furniture*, Bonanza, 1989

Albert Jackson and David Day, *Collins Complete Woodworker's Manual*, HarperCollins, London, 1989

Ernest Joyce, *The Technique of Furniture Making*, B.T. Batsford Ltd, London, 2003

Ray Key, *The Woodturner's Workbook*, B.T. Batsford Ltd, London, 1994

Nigel Lofthouse, *The Woodworker's Pocket Palette*, B.T. Batsford Ltd, London, 1993

Jack Metcalfe and John Apps, *The Marquetry Course*, B.T. Batsford Ltd, London, 2003

Frederick Oughton, *The Complete Manual of Wood Finishing*, Stobart Davies Ltd, London, 1982

Alan Peters, *Cabinet Making: The Professional Approach*, Stobart and Son Ltd, London, 1984

David Regester, *Woodturning: Step-by-Step*, B.T. Batsford Ltd, London, 1993

David Regester, *Turning Boxes and Spindles: Step-by-Step*, B.T. Batsford Ltd, London, 1994

David Regester, *Turning Bowls: Step-by-Step*, B.T. Batsford Ltd, London, 1994

Ray Tabor, *Green Woodworking Pattern Book*, B.T. Batsford Ltd, London, 2005

Alan Waterhouse and Philippa Barstow, *French Polishing*, B.T. Batsford Ltd, London, 1993

INDEX

Page numbers in *italics* refer to photographs and illustrations

Abrasives 98–99
  Aluminium Oxide 98, *99*
  Comparative grades 99
  Denibbing 98
  Garnet 98, *99*
  Glass paper 98, *99*
  Self-lubricating silicon carbide paper 98
  Silicon carbide paper 99
  Wet and dry *98*, *99*
Adhesives 93
  Impact/contact adhesives 93
  PVA 93
  Scotch/pearl glue 93
  Two-part adhesives 93
Air drying 10
Ash, American White 13
Assembling 89–99
  Checking for square 90
  Clamping block 89
  Complex projects 91
  Correcting out-of-square frames 92
  Dovetail joints 93
  Dry assembly 89
  Edge-jointed boards 92
  Holding awkward shapes 93
  Keeping frames square 55
  Mitred frames 57
  Simple frames 90

Backing off 59
Balanced construction 15
Beech, European 12
Bedside cabinet 142–147
Bench hook 27
Bench stop 56
Bevel 74
Blockboard 15
Bow (warping) 14
Bookcase 118–125
Brace 46, *46*
  How to use 48
Bradawl 47, *47*

Cabinet backs, fitting 145
Cabinet scraper *34*, 34–36
  Gooseneck scraper *34*

Sharpening 35–36
Using 34
Callipers 22, *22*
Cap iron 38
Carcase 21
Catches *147*
  Ball catch *147*
  Double ball catch *147*
  Magnetic catch *147*
Cauls 56
Chamfers 74
Chest 134–141
Cherry, Pennsylvanian Black 13
Child's desk 126–133
Chipboard 15, 126
Chisels
  Bevel-edged chisels 42, *42*
  Firmer chisel 42, *42*
  Handles
    Carver *42*, 43
    Moulded/oval *42*, 43
    Octagonal 43
  How to use 44
  Mortise chisel 43
Chocks 10
Clamps
  Bench hold fast clamps 54
  Clamp heads *54*, *55*
  Fast-action clamps *54*, 55
  Flat bar sash clamps *54*, 55
  G-clamp 54, *54*
  Holding awkward shapes 57
  Holding mitred frames 57
  T-bar sash clamp *54*, 55
  Web clamp 57
Cleaning up 94–95
  Dovetail joints 95
  Edge-jointed boards 95
  Simple frame 94
  Surface 95
  Top edge 95
Clearance hole 47
Combination square *19*, 20, 23
Coping saw 27
Cup (warping) 14
Craft knife 21
Creep (chisel) 146
Cutting board 88
Cutting gauge 21, *22*

Cutting lists 111
Dead knots 15
Dents, repairing 97
Depth gauge 21
Douglas fir 12
Dividers 22, *22*
Doors
  Fitting a door panel 149
  Hanging 146
  Making and fitting 146
Dovetail gauge *22*, 23
Dovetail nailing 79
Dovetails and pins 88
Drawers
  Cock beaded 155
  Fitting 154
  Inset 155
  Making 154
  Overlapping false front 155
Draw filing 34
Drill bits
  Auger bit 47
  Centre bit 47
  Countersink 47
  Expansive bit 47
  Insertion and removal of 47
  Plug cutter 47
  Twist drill 47
Dust panels 129

Fibreboard 15
Finishing 100–107
  Brushes 105, 107
  Burnishing cream 105
  Carnauba wax 104
  Chemical stain 107
  Colour toning 107
  Deciding what to use 100
  Denibbing 100, 104
    00 flour paper 105
    Materials used for
    Micromesh 105
    Pumice powder 105
    Rottonstone 105
    Self-lubricating silicon carbide paper 105
    Steel wool 105
    Wet and dry paper 105
  French polish 103, 104
    Grain fillers 103
    How to polish 100, 101
  Lacquer 104

Lint-free cotton 104, 107
Looking after furniture 105
Modified French polish 103
Oil-based stain 106
Oil finishes 102
Polishes 100
Polishing mop 100, 104
Raising the grain 107
Removing water marks 105
Removing ring marks 105
Repairing scratch marks 105
Reviving furniture 105
Sanding sealer 103
Spirit stain 106
Traditional wood stain 100, 106
Water-based stain 106
Waxing barewood 102
Waxing sealed wood 102
Wood stains 100, 106
Varnish 104
Folding rule *19*, 21

Gimlet 47, *47*
Glue blocks 66
Gluing up 90
Grading, timber 15
Grinding angle 59
Grooves 32
Grooving wood 129

Hammers 39
  Ball pein *39*, 40
  Claw 39, 40
  Cross pein (Warrington) *39*, 40
  Pin *39*, 40
  Telephone 39, 40
Hand drill 46, *46*
  How to use 48
Handles 40, *147*
  Cabinet handle *147*
  Domed knob handle *147*
  Drop handle *147*
  Flat knob handle *147*
  Fretted plate handle *147*
  Plate handle *147*
  Ring handle *147*
Hardboard 15
Hardwoods 13, 14
Haunching joints 137

Hinges 146, *147*
  Butt hinges *147*
  Fitting 146
  H-hinge *147*
  Snake hinge *147*
Homogenous 15
Honing 59, 61
Honing guide 33
Hygroscopic 10

Inlay 70
Iroko 13

Joints 68–69
  Bare-faced joints 66
  Butt joint 69
  Bridle joint *68*, 84
    Corner bridle joint 84
    T-bridle joint 84
    Under bridle joint 84
  Cutting and fitting joints 76–88
    Butt joints 79
    Dovetail joint 85–88
    Dowel joints 78
    Edge joints 79
    Housing joint 84, 85
    Lapped dovetail joint 88
    Mitres 77
    Mortise and tenon joints 80
      Cleaning up 82
      Cutting the mortise 82
      Cutting the tenon 81
  Dovetail joint *68*, 69, 85, 86, 87, 88
  Dovetail halving joint 69
  Dowel joint 69
  Halving joint *68*, 69
    Cross halving joint 83
    Corner halving joint 83
    T-halving joint 83
  Housing joint *68*, 85
    Bare-faced housing joint 85
    Dovetail housing joint 85
    Stopped housing joint 85
    Through-housing joint 85
  Lap joint 69
  Mitre joint 21, 69
  Mortise and tenon joint *68*, 69, 80
    Loose wedge *80*
    Moulded groove frame 80
    Stopped 80
    Rebate joint 69
    Through 80
  Tongue-and-groove joint 38, 69
  Under bridle joint 84

Kerf 27
Kiln drying 10

Lamin board 15
Live knots 15

Machine cutter marks 96
Mahogany, Brazilian 13
Maple, hard (Hard rock) 13
Maple, sugar 13
Mallets 39, *39*, 41, 45
Marking knife 21, 23
Marking gauge 21, *22*, 23
  Setting 67, *67*
Measuring and marking out 18, 64–69
  Bridle joint 84
  Cross halving joint 83
  Dovetail joint 85
  Dowel 78
  External dimensions 20
  Halving joint 83
  Housing joint 84
  Internal dimensions 20
  Mitre 77
  Mortise and tenon 80
    Twin stub tenon 144
  Setting a marking gauge 67
  Shoulder line 66
Medium board 15
Medium density fibre board (MDF) 15, 126
Mitre box *28*, 29
  Using 77
Moulding edges 75
Mouldings
  Bullnose *123*
  Flute *123*
  Ogee *123*
  Ovolo *123*

Pencil round *123*
Quirk bead *123*
Reed *123*

Nails 41
    Dovetail nailing 41
    Lost head wire 41, *41*
    Oval wire 41, *41*
    Panel pin 41
    Removing 41
    Round wire 41, *41*
Nominal sizes 15

Oak, American White 13
Orbital sander 98

Panel gauge 70
Panels
    Making and fitting 139
    Raised and fielded 139
Parana pine 12
Paraffin wax 88
Paring horizontal 44, *44*
Paring vertical 44, *44*
Pellets 49
Pilot hole 47
Pine, European Redwood 12
Plain sawn 14
Planed all round (PAR) 14
Planed square edge (PSE) 14
Planes
    Block plane *30*, 31
    Combination plane 32, *32*, 75
    Fore plane *30*, 31
    Jack plane *30*, 31
    Jointer plane *30*, 31
    Plough plane 32, *32*
    Rebate plane 32, *32*
    Router plane *32*, 33
    Scraper plane 32, *32*, 34
    Shoulder plane 32, *32*
    Smoothing plane *30*, 31
    Spoke shave *32*, 33
    Try plane *30*, 31
Planing 70–74
    Decorative mouldings 74
    Edge jointed boards 79

End grain 74
Grooving wood 129
Planing boards flat 70, 71
Squaring an edge 72, 73
Traverse planing 71
Plywood 15, 126
Polishing 100
Profile gauge 21

Quartersawn 14

Rebate 32, 38
Redwood, European 12
Ring porous 15
Rock maple 13
Rounds 74, 75

Safety equipment 11
Sanding 96
Sanding mouldings 75
Saws 24–29
    Aggressive geometry teeth 24, *25*
    Bead saw 24
    Coping saw 28, *28*, 29
    Crosscut saw 24
    Crosscut teeth 24, *25*
    Dovetail saw 24, *25*
    Fleam teeth 25
    Fret saw 28, *28*, 29
    Gentleman's back saw 28, *28*
    Handsaw 24, *25*
    Hardpoint teeth 24
    Measuring tooth size 25
    Panel saw 24
    Rip saw 24
    Rip saw teeth 24, *25*
    Set 27
    Tenon saw 24, 25
    Universal teeth 25
Sawing
    Cutting to size 9
    Problem solving 27
    Using a back saw 26, *26*
    Using a coping saw 29
    Using a handsaw 26
Saw handles

Closed grip 27
Offset 27
Pistol 27
Straight 27
Scraper *see also* Cabinet scraper
Scratch stock 75
Screwdrivers 50–51
    Cabinet handle *51*
    Cranked/offset 51
    Flared tip *51*
    Long reach 51, *51*
    Parallel tip *51*
    Precision instrument 51, *51*
    Stubby 51, *51*
Screws 52–53
    Countersunk 52
    Crosspoint 52
    Fitting components 53
    Head type and shape 52
    Inserting 53
    Raised head 52
    Round head 52
    Screw size 52
    Slotted 52
    Traditional screw thread 52
    Twin thread 52
Secondary conditioning 10
Sharpening
    Chisels 60
    Lubricants 61
    Plane blade 58, *58*, 59
    Stone 60, 61, *61*
Sheet materials
    Cutting 9
    Types 15
    Working in 129
Shooting board 70
Shoulder 21, 27
Sliding bevel *19*, 21
Softboard 15
Softwood 12
Southern Yellow Pine 12
Spirit level *22*, 23
Splays 74
Splits 98

Repairing 97
Spring (warping) 14
Squaring rod *89*, 90
Staining 106
Steel rule *19*, 20, 23
Sticking lathes 10
Stile 66
Stock 21, 66
Stopped rebate 32
Stoppers 97
    Beaumontage 97
    Powder-based 97
    Shellec sticks 97
    Wax sticks 97
Strop 60
Surform 37, *37*, 38

Table with drawer 150–157
Tape measure *19*, 23
Teak 14
Tops
    Fitting 121
    Stretcher plates 121
    Wooden buttons 121
Torn grain 34, 96
Trammel 21
Trench 38, 88
Trimming knife 21, *22*, 23
Try square *19*, 21, 23
Twist (warping) 14

Vials 21
Vice *54*, 56

Walnut, American Black 14
Waney edge 12, 21, 23
Warping 10, 14
Western Red Cedar 13
Whitewood, European 12
Winding sticks 70
Woodbench 11
Wood fillers 97
Wood, how to look after 9
Working drawings 110
    Bedside cabinet 148–149
    Bookcase 124–125
    Chest 140–141
    Child's desk 130–133

Small table with drawer 156–157
Workbench 116–117

Yellow pine, Quebec 12